WHY DID MY SAVIOR COME TO EARTH?

WHY DID MY SAVIOR COME TO EARTH?

Jim Faughn

START2FINISH

ISBN-10: 1944704329
ISBN-13: 978-1944704322

Published by Start2Finish
Fort Worth, Texas 76244
www.start2finish.org

Printed in the United States of America

Cover Design: Josh Feit, Evangela.com

CONTENTS

INTRODUCTION

I remember the day when two passages of scripture seemed to have entered my mind at the same time. Both of them had to do with a reason the Lord gave for His earthly mission. I began to wonder how many times He said something like that. I further began to wonder about the application(s) that could be made for my life and the lives of others.

This book is the result of some of my "wonderings." It is not intended to be a doctrinal or theological book (though I guess doctrine and theology are in it). Rather, the book is intended to be helpful. It is my prayer that it will help all of us have a better understanding of our Lord and His work. It is also my prayer that it will cause us to love Him even more than we do now and to be more dedicated to His cause than might presently be the case.

1

"HE WHO CAME DOWN FROM HEAVEN"

JOHN 3:13

It appears to have been a private conversation between two men. Whether or not he wore the clothing that evening that would have identified him as a Pharisee and a member of the Sanhedrin, Nicodemus was, in fact, both.

It will not be our purpose here to add to the speculation about why he may have chosen to come to Jesus at night. Nor shall we speculate as to exactly how much faith he had in Jesus. Our purpose here is to focus on the other party in this conversation. Jesus, the master teacher, was able to answer the unasked question. His mention of the need to be born again brought about a discussion and some important teaching from our Lord. The first eighteen verses of John 3 contain this material.

These verses also record the first time (chronologically) when our Lord gave any hint as to the answer to the question, "Why did my Savior come to earth?" He would expand upon this first answer during His earthly ministry and would give additional insight into the reason for His incarnation. We hope to explore some of the Lord's other statements about this in succeeding chapters.

However, what He says in John 3 in the actual statement and its context should give us much to consider and appreciate. The material which follows does not exhaust or "touch the hem of the garment" of all that could be said about this marvelous passage.

It is hoped that it will cause us to dig a little deeper into God's Book and love even more deeply His Son. Only three of the many points that could be discussed will be dealt with in this chapter.

HIS "ORIGIN"

The fact that the word "origin" is in quotation marks is not an accident. The fact is that "He who came down from heaven" had no origin.

Every attempt that is used to explain eternity seems to fall woefully short. It is beyond getting one's brain around the idea that anything or anybody could have no beginning and will have no end. As much as we sometimes hesitate to think of our own departure from this life, we are used to the idea of things having a beginning and an ending. This is true whether we are considering a song, a book, a television show, a theatrical production, a nation's history, or our own lives.

It seems that, just about the time when we get anywhere near "comfortable" with the concept that we will exist somewhere forever, we come face to face with another truth; Deity, like us, has no ending, but, unlike us, had no beginning. To state this truth in another way, the Bible teaches that before the beginning, there was God. We might not be able to explain it even to ourselves, but the opening words of God's grand Book tell of what He did "in the beginning" (Gen. 1:1).

If the objection would be raised that this wording might mean that He, too, had a beginning, consideration needs to be given to those passages which speak of things in which He was involved before the beginning. For example, the church was part of His "eternal purpose" (Eph. 3:10-11).

God's plan for redeeming mankind "in Christ" was not an afterthought. Consideration should be given to Paul's inspired words as found in Ephesians 1:3-4: "Blessed be the God and Father of our Lord Jesus Christ, who hath blessed us with all spiritual blessings in heavenly places in Christ: According as he hath chosen us in him before the foundation of the world, that we should be holy and without blame before him in love."

There exists the possibility that our Lord may not have needed to exist before the creation in order for the plan to be in place. Peter's pen seems to answer this question, though, by stating that Christ was "foreordained before the foundation of the world, but was manifest in these last times for you" (1 Pet. 1:19-20). It is interesting and important to notice that the Messiah was "manifest" or that He "has appeared" (NASU). Nowhere is it taught that the plan existed before the One existed who would implement the plan.

As the beloved apostle John began his inspired account of our Lord's person and mission, he informed his readers that "the Word" which "was made flesh" was "in the beginning with God" and "was God" (John 1:1-2, 14). Although this truth is denied by at least one very zealous religious group, the fact remains that the One to whom Nicodemus was speaking in John 3 has no origin.

It is not true, as that group teaches and as they have "edited" their Bibles to say, that Jesus was a created being. He is not, as their Bible has it, "a god," (John 1:1; *New World Translation of the Christian Greek Scriptures*). It is also not true, as that same Bible states in Colossians 1:16 that "by means of him all *other* things were created" (emphasis added).

John affirms, and the Bible repeatedly teaches, that the One having that conversation with Nicodemus was, and is, Deity. He was not an angel who left heaven to come to earth. He was and is part of the Godhead! He was the One to whom the Father spoke and referred to as God in Hebrews 1:8! "But to the Son He says: 'Your throne, O God, is forever and ever; a scepter of righteousness is the scepter of Your kingdom.'"

Since John affirms the Deity of Jesus, it should not surprise us to learn some of the other things we find in chapter one of his gospel. Along with His creative power, John mentions, among other things, the truth that life is to be found "in Him" (v. 4); that He is "full of grace and truth" (v. 14); and that He makes the Father known (v. 18).

There is a very intriguing passage found in Hebrews 10. In a sense, "the curtain is lifted" on a conversation that took place before our Savior came to earth. In verses 5-10, we learn that it is not true, as one song suggests, that "they searched through heaven and found a savior." Rather, our Lord willingly left the glory he had with His Father before the world existed (cf. John 17:5) in order to come to earth to offer the ultimate and only adequate sacrifice for sin.

In the inspired words of the apostle Paul found in Philippians 2:6, He is described as both "being in the form of God" and being "equal with God." With amazement and appreciation, we read the following verses which inform us that He "made himself of no reputation, and took upon him the form of a servant, and was made in the likeness of men: And being found in fashion as a man, he humbled himself, and became obedient unto death, even the death of the cross" (vv. 7-8).

Think of it! On that dark day so very long ago, the One being cruelly executed between two common criminals was the most uncommon of all who have ever walked the earth. Thomas spoke the truth when he bowed to Jesus and said, "My Lord and My God" (John 20:28).

HIS NATURE

It is worth noting that Jesus often referred to Himself in the third person. On five occasions, He referred to Himself as "the Son of God." However, He was more apt to call Himself "the Son of Man." In fact, we find Him using the expression "Son of Man" over eighty times in the Gospels, while referring to Himself as the "Son of God" only five times.

The fact that Jesus is "the Son of Man," of course, has reference to a prophecy that is almost as old as the human race. In Genesis 3:15, God said that the seed of woman would ultimately defeat Satan.

When all of the debate about Isaiah 7:14 dies down, the fact remains that it is predicted that "a virgin shall conceive, and bear a son, and shall call his name Immanuel." Matthew's gospel connects this to the birth of Jesus and adds the information that Immanuel "is translated, God with us" (Matt. 1:23).

The fulfillment of prophecies is an exciting and rewarding study. Some have made a life's work of studying all of the prophecies that were (and are) fulfilled by our Lord. It is also rewarding to consider that "we have not an high priest which cannot be touched with the feeling of our infirmities; but was in all points tempted like as we are, yet without sin" (Heb. 4:15). When we sing the song that asks and answers the question, "Does Jesus Care?" we can be sure that He does. We can be sure of that, in part, because it is "He who came down from heaven" (John 3:13).

We have already briefly considered the passage found in Philippians 2 which affirms that the Messiah came "in the likeness of men" (v. 7) and was "found in appearance as a man" (v. 8). Some might object, or at least wonder, if these two expressions would leave room for the idea that Jesus never really was a man, but that He just appeared to be a man.

This idea might even seem to find support in Hebrews 2:14 where it is stated that He "took part" in flesh and blood. Maybe, some might reason or wonder, He never really became man. That same verse destroys that notion when it teaches that all of mankind are "partakers of flesh and blood." Jesus was just as much human as you and I are.

However, that fact, at least to this author, is not the most amazing truth to be learned from Hebrews 2. In verse 11, we are told that Jesus and His followers "are all of one." We are not just considering our Lord's desire that all of us would be one (cf. John 17:21). Hebrews 2:11 states that "He who sanctifies and those who are being sanctified are all *of* one" (emphasis added). We have the same Father!

Does that amaze and humble you at the same time? If so, consider the rest of that verse wherein we learn that Christ "is not ashamed to call them (us) brethren." It is nothing short of amazing that, because He has been one of us, He can and does understand more than we can imagine and can actually refer to us as brethren.

This is especially true when we remember that He is not just one of us. He is also the Son of God. One of the fascinating features of the exchange between Jesus and the Jewish high priest as recorded in Matthew 26:63-64 is the connection that Jesus made between the two concepts of His being both the "Son of God" (v. 63) and the "Son of Man" (v. 64). He accepted the first "title" and made reference to Himself with the second.

In His conversation with Nicodemus, He referred to Himself as both "the Son of Man" and "the Son of God" (vv. 14, 18). Both of these appellations refer to His nature and both of them refer to the reason why "He... came down from heaven" (John 3:13).

HIS MISSION

To turn this discussion into a study of our Lord's mission while on earth would be a worthy (but extremely lengthy) effort. To try to tie together all the prophecies, fulfillments, works of our Lord, applications for our lives, etc. would require volumes. Even inspired writers did not tell us everything that could have been told. In the inspired closing of John's gospel, he informs us that "there are also many other things that Jesus did, which if they were written one by one, I suppose that even the world itself could not contain the books that would be written. Amen" (John 21:25).

Accordingly, this discussion will be limited to four points that present themselves in different forms in the text of John 3. Hopefully, these four points will whet our appetites for further study and examination.

First, it is important to notice that Jesus asked Nicodemus a revealing question in verse 10: "Are you a teacher of Israel, and do not know these things?" The strong implication is that those who knew the Old Testament Law and the prophecies contained in the Old Testament should have been the very ones who would recognize Him.

However, two things become very apparent as we read the gospel accounts of Jesus' earthly ministry. The first is that His most adamant antagonists came from the "religious class." Repeatedly, they attacked Him in almost every conceivable way and were, in fact, among the major players leading to His crucifixion. It does not appear that Nicodemus was one of that number wanting to put Him to death.

However, it does appear that Nicodemus was like many others whose actions are questioned and sometimes criticized by Jesus. This is the second apparent aspect of our Lord's interaction with the Jews. Over and over again, He questions, criticizes, and/or points out the almost total lack of understanding on the part of those who should have known the scriptures.

One part of His mission, then, was—

the fulfillment of Old Testament scriptures.

Very often we find Jesus or one of His "inspired biographers" pointing out that one of His actions, teachings, etc. was done "that it might be fulfilled," "that the scriptures might be fulfilled," etc.

When He said to the people in His hometown of Nazareth, "Today this Scripture is fulfilled in your hearing" (Luke 4:21), that was not the last time that something like that would happen. At His appearance to His disciples after His resurrection, He told them, "These are the words which I spake unto you, while I was yet with you, that all things must be fulfilled, which were written in the law of Moses, and in the prophets, and in the psalms, concerning me" (Luke 24:44).

Some of those great sermons we can read in the book of Acts are built, at least in part, on the fact that Jesus fulfilled the Old Testament prophecies. Some great sermons could and should be preached today on that same subject.

Jesus also indicated to Nicodemus that He came to "tell you heavenly things" (John 3:13). He did just that. Not only did He reveal the Father to us, He also revealed to us how His Father views matters. We might not know from His teaching or from any other teaching in God's word exactly what heaven looks like, but we do know how heaven looks at us. Accordingly, another part of His mission was—

to reveal heavenly truths.

What follows is a very short list containing some of these truths:

- Material and temporal matters should not be of as great a concern to us as eternal and spiritual matters.
- One soul is worth more than the entire world.
- Forgiving each other is not an option, but an absolute necessity.
- What the world sees as important is actually of very little importance.
- Seemingly small acts (like giving a cup of cold water) do not go unnoticed.
- The way up is down.
- Service is much more important than position.
- Time needs to be spent with "the undesirables."

Again, these are but a few of the life-changing truths that can be learned and should be put into practice by all who wear the name "Christian." Part of our growth as Christians needs to attempt to view things from God's perspective, not ours.

The conversation with Nicodemus was not yet complete. The conversation demonstrates that another part of the mission of Jesus had to do with—

the eternally important subject of salvation.

We plan to look at that subject in more detail later in this book when we consider one of those statements of Jesus when He says, "the Son of Man has come to seek and to save that which was lost" (Luke 19:10).

At this time, let us briefly consider the following from John 3. Two different and distinct fates await people at the end of our time here on earth. Jesus uses the word "perish" to refer to one and "everlasting life" to refer to the other (v. 16). These truths are "fleshed out" in other portions of scripture.

Other Scriptures also "flesh out" all that is involved in our salvation. Suffice it to say at this time that it becomes very apparent from this account we have been considering that our only hope is Jesus. In Him, we find a proper relationship with God. If we are not in that relationship, we are "condemned already" (v. 18).

This may be the third part of this discussion we are looking at here, but it deserves first place in our priorities. It needs to be remembered that He was the one who asked: "For what profit is it to a man if he gains the whole world and loses his own soul? Or what will a man give in exchange for his soul?" (Matt. 16:26)

Finally, let us notice that the subject of light plays a role in Jesus' discussion with Nicodemus. His mission involved—

bringing light into a very dark world.

It will be remembered that, in his "introduction," John states that "in Him was life, and the life was the light of men" (John 1:4). Sadly, he further records that "the light shines in the darkness, and the darkness did not comprehend it" (John 1:5). How many today can be described in the same way? How many today do not come to the light because their deeds are evil? How many love darkness rather than light (cf. John 3:19-20)?

Because we live in a world that seems to be increasingly dark, it may be tempting for a Christian to lose heart. It might be helpful to remember that the One who said, "As long as I am in the world, I am the light of the world" (John 9:5) was the same One who was ridiculed, ostracized, spat upon, and crucified. It will be remembered that, later in John's gospel, Jesus told the eleven apostles who were still with Him after the departure of Judas, "If the world hates you, keep in mind that it hated me first" (John 15:18). When this statement is read in its context, it should be noted that this was not meant to be a fatalistic or pessimistic statement. Rather, in that same context, the Lord was promising to those men the Holy Spirit as their Comforter.

To be sure, Jesus was being realistic with them. At the same time, He did not want them—or us—to lose heart.

It might be appropriate to conclude this chapter with the words of one who, at first, was one of those walking in darkness. Later, he became a sincere follower of Jesus and a most effective evangelist. The fact that there was much darkness around him did not deter him from his mission. That is demonstrated in these words:

> Therefore, since we have this ministry, as we have received mercy, we do not lose heart. But we have renounced the hidden things of shame, not walking in craftiness nor handling the word of God deceitfully, but by the manifestation of the truth commending ourselves to every man's conscience in the sight of God. But even if our gospel is veiled, it is veiled to those who are perishing, whose minds the god of this age has blinded, who do not believe, lest the light of the gospel of the glory of Christ, who is the image of God, should shine on them. For we do not preach ourselves, but Christ Jesus the Lord, and ourselves your bondservants for Jesus' sake. For it is the God who commanded light to shine out of darkness, who has shone in our hearts to give the light of the knowledge of the glory of God in the face of Jesus Christ. But we have this treasure in earthen vessels, that the excellence of the power may be of God and not of us. We are hard-

> pressed on every side, yet not crushed; we are perplexed, but not in despair; persecuted, but not forsaken; struck down, but not destroyed — always carrying about in the body the dying of the Lord Jesus, that the life of Jesus also may be manifested in our body.
>
> 2 Corinthians 4:1-10

Hopefully, each of us will determine to follow Paul's example and will be in our time what we should be. Individually, we are called to be Christians. Collectively, we are to comprise the body of Christ. May God help us to fulfill our mission and bring glory to the One who came down from heaven.

2

"I AM COME IN MY FATHER'S NAME"

JOHN 5:43

There he stood. He looked young enough to be my son who, at that time, was about thirty years of age. In fact, this young man who was standing on my doorstep looked younger than my son. He tried in every way to assure me of his credentials. He told me that he represented a particular insurance company. He wore a name tag that identified him as a representative for that company. He even told me who his manager was. Apparently he knew that it was important to establish some credibility before he gave me some information I needed.

I could have asked my son. I've known him a lot longer. He is even (I think) older than this young man. I have no doubt about his honesty and integrity. There is only one problem. My son does not pretend to have the information about this particular subject that this young man had.

If I was going to find out anything about this insurance company, I was going to have to rely on the knowledge and the credentials of this young man standing in my doorway. I might have a lot more experience and knowledge about some things, but not this.

Years ago, in a place foreign to most of us, another young man claimed to have information vitally needed by the people of His day. In fact, His claim was to have information for people of every age and time.

Many of His day did not readily accept His credentials. This was definitely true concerning those who (at least) appeared to be older than He was and who thought they knew more about the subject He seemed to spend most of His time discussing. The information and the "insurance" He offered had (has) eternal consequences.

He had already identified Himself as "He who came from heaven" (John 3:13). Among other things, that statement meant that His existence did not begin when His mother conceived Him. In effect, it helped establish His Deity.

The immediate background for this statement has to do with His healing the man at the pool of Bethesda. As had already been the case before and would be many times in the future, this caused the Jewish leaders of His day some real problems.

First, they were very concerned about the fact that He had healed a man on the Sabbath day. This was not an isolated incident, concern, or controversy. At least on the occasions listed below, as well as the one recorded in John 5, Jesus performed a miracle on that sacred day. It was not unusual for controversy to accompany these incidents:

- Casting an unclean spirit out of a man in a synagogue in Capernaum (Mark 1:21-28)
- Healing Simon's wife's mother (Luke 4:31, 38-39)
- Healing the man with a withered hand (Luke 6:6-11)
- Healing the woman with an infirmity for eighteen years (Luke 13:11-17)
- Healing a man with dropsy (Luke 14:1-6)
- Restoring sight to a man blind from birth (John 9:1-41)

However, the fact that Jesus healed on the Sabbath was not the only bone of contention this time. His credentials were being questioned. Specifically, He had made some statements about His relationship with God. These statements were not merely a source of concern for the Jewish leaders. These statements angered them.

Consider, in particular, our Lord's statement and the reaction of the Jewish leaders in verses 17-18: "But Jesus answered them, 'My Father has been working until now, and I have been working. Therefore the Jews sought all the more to kill Him, because He not only broke the Sabbath but also said that God was His Father, making Himself equal with God."

In the continuing answer to His critics, Jesus presented no less than five pieces of evidence to substantiate His claims concerning His relationship with the Father. It is almost as if He was asking a witness to testify at a trial.

First, He realized the futility (in their eyes) of making the claim Himself. That seems to be the meaning of these words: "If I bear witness of myself, my witness is not true" (v. 31).

Second, He "called to the stand" John the Baptist. Consider what is said about John in verses 33-35. It is interesting that Jesus reminds His critics that "you sent for John" (v. 33). Maybe the adage that tells us not to ask if we really don't want to know would have been appropriate for the Jews to heed on this occasion.

The third witness Jesus relies on has to do with the works He was doing. The weight of that evidence can be seen if we remember the conversation that Jesus had with Nicodemus. Interestingly enough, Nicodemus' first statement to Jesus was, "Rabbi, we know that you are a teacher from God, for no man can do these miracles that you do, *except God is with Him*" (John 3:2, emphasis added).

Even in our day, it is helpful to remember the purpose of the works of Jesus. In the same Gospel of John, we read the words: "And truly Jesus did many other signs in the presence of His disciples, which are not written in this book; but these are written that you may believe that Jesus is the Christ, the Son of God, and that believing you may have life in His name

(John 20:30-31).

If this were one of those dramatized courtroom scenes, we could imagine the stir caused by the mention of the next witness. We can only imagine what might have been going through the minds of the self-proclaimed "keepers of the faith" when they heard Jesus say, "And the Father Himself, who sent Me, has testified of Me" (John 5:43). What could be more devastating than this? How would one go about trying to "trump" the testimony of Jesus, John the Baptist, the miracles and other works of Jesus, and the Father Himself?

The answer to that question may be found as one considers how important the scriptures were to these Jewish leaders. It could be argued that the scriptures were of utmost importance. Many of them devoted their lives to searching the scriptures. They were experts in minutia but had totally forgotten people. The entire debate about healing on the Sabbath demonstrated this.

Not only had they forgotten people, but they had also totally missed the big picture. What a slap in the face they must have felt when they were challenged in this manner: "You search the Scriptures, for in them you think you have eternal life; and these are they which testify of Me" (John 5:39). Readers of God's Word today would do well to learn from their mistake. If we fail to see Jesus in both the Old Testament and the New Testament, we desperately need to readjust our focus!

Surely, their focus and their attention was challenged when Jesus said, "I have come in My Father's name, and you do not receive Me; if another comes in his own name, him you will receive. How can you believe, who receive honor from one another, and do not seek the honor that comes from the only God?" (John 5:43-44).

What did that mean? How serious was it that they did not receive Him? What are the implications of receiving those who come in their own name? These are some of the questions which will occupy our attention for the remainder of this chapter.

Considerable space could be devoted to a study of the phrase "in the name of." For our study here, we will confine our discussion to three passages from the Old Testament.

The first of these is found in the context of a major confrontation between God's people and their enemies. This battle would be decided by two combatants. Goliath of Gath arrogantly and rudely said to the young boy standing in front of him, "Come to me, and I will give your flesh to the birds of the air and the beasts of the field" (1 Sam. 17:44)!

David's answer is as instructive as it is confident:

> You come to me with a sword, with a spear, and with a javelin. But I come to you in the name of the LORD of hosts, the God of the armies of Israel, whom you have defied. This day the LORD will deliver you into my hand, and I will strike you and take your head from you. And this day I will give the carcasses of the camp of the Philistines to the birds of the air and the wild beasts of the earth, that all the earth may know that there is a God in Israel. Then all this assembly shall know that the LORD does not save with sword and spear; for the battle is the LORD's, and He will give you into our hands.
>
> 1 Samuel 17:45-47

If this statement means anything at all, it is a statement concerning God's power. David most surely demonstrated a deep faith in God's power. More than that, he believed strongly that those who were doing His will could accomplish what the Father wanted to have accomplished, even in the face of terrific odds.

Our second Old Testament passage does not mention God, but it is, nevertheless, very instructive about the phrase "in the name of." It involves the intrigue surrounding Haman's attempt to rid his society (and maybe the world) of the Jews. In Esther 3, he asked King Ahasuerus for permission to have a law written to that effect. The details about how Haman received that permission and how his wishes were carried out are interesting.

First, Ahasuerus allowed Haman to use his signet ring (cf. v. 10). It could be argued that a king's ring was seen as almost, if not altogether, important as his scepter, crown, and/or throne. When a document was sealed by making an imprint of the ring in wax, whatever the document said was a "done deal." The ring and the seal meant, in effect, "This document was written by, and carries with it, the authority of the king."

Along with the sealing of the law with the king's ring, it is definitely stated that, "in the name of King Ahasuerus it was written" (Esth. 3:12). "In the name of" is not just a statement about power. It is also a statement concerning authority.

Our third passage will actually be the first passage in the Bible where we can read the phrase "in the name of." That passage is Deuteronomy 18. We usually think of that chapter as the one in which we find God informing Moses that, someday, He would raise up another Prophet like Moses (vv. 15, 18). It would be God's choice as to the timing of that event (cf. Gal. 4:4). He alone would determine the identity of that Prophet. Thus, His power would be demonstrated.

It is also made clear in this passage that God's commands were to be taught. God said, "I will raise up for them a Prophet like you from among their brethren, and will put My words in His mouth, and He shall speak to them all that I command Him" (Deut. 18:18). This speaks to His authority.

However, it is God's "test" that links this passage with John 5 and with us. It may also be the most challenging of the three concepts. It may be possible to at least give "lip service" to the idea that God has both power and authority and still not pass His "test."

God made it clear in Deuteronomy 18 that some would not pass His test. Some spokesmen would not pass the test. Likewise, some hearers would not pass the test. The spokesmen who would not pass the test would be anybody who "presumes to speak a word in My name, which I have not commanded him to speak, or who speaks in the name of other gods" (Deut. 18:20). Everybody then who claimed to speak for God did not, in fact, do so.

At the same time, there were hearers who would not pass an important test. They would hear a message with the qualities of both God's power and His authority, but would not heed it.

In case there could be any question as to who this Prophet was that is predicted in Deuteronomy 18, all such questions are answered in light of the use of the term "that Prophet" or "the Prophet" by John the Baptist when he was being questioned by some priests and Levites (John 1:20). It does not take much thought or research to realize that Jesus is seen as the fulfillment of the prophecy in Deuteronomy 18.

Not only was Jesus the fulfillment of that prophecy, but also the incident recorded in John 5 is a fulfillment of the idea that some of His day failed God's test. Consider carefully this statement as recorded in John 5:43-44: "I have come in My Father's name, and you do not receive Me; if another comes in his own name, him you will receive. How can you believe, who receive honor from one another, and do not seek the honor that comes from the only God?"

Doesn't Jesus' criticism of those Jews sound much like what it said in Deuteronomy 18? Doesn't it sound like there would be those who could accurately be labeled as "false prophets"? Doesn't it also sound like there were those who would rather believe the false prophets than to accept the Messiah?

Consider carefully the phrase in verse 43 wherein Jesus mentioned "another (who) comes in his own name." Compare that with the following quotation found on page 113 of Brother Guy N. Woods' volume, *A Commentary on the Gospel of John*: "The German theologian, Schudt, quoting an earlier Jewish writer, says that at least sixty-four pretenders to the messiahship had been accepted by the Jews at one time or another."

Think about that for a minute. If these sixty-four pretenders claimed to be the Messiah, they did not, at the same time, claim to have come in their own name. Their claims that they were the Messiah did not make it so. In effect, they (as some might say) "flunked the test big time." Does this have any application in our day, or are we just looking at another interesting and important quote of our Lord? It seems that some questions are in order.

First, how many of the religious groups today do not claim to be pointing people to God? Is it not true that the entire concept of denominationalism stands or falls on the claim that "we are all going to the same place"?

Second, does such a claim hold up just because it is made or should we subject this claim to some sort of test? Would it not be wise for us to "check out the credentials" of any and all groups and spokesmen who claim to represent God?

It seems that we would do well to ask the same question Jesus asked some of His detractors in Luke 20 concerning the baptism of John. His interest was in getting them to take a position about whether that baptism was "from heaven or from men" (v. 4).

We are admonished to "...test the spirits, whether they are of God" (1 John 4:1). Further, we are informed that even on the Day of Judgment, there will be those who will claim to have represented Jesus, but who, in fact, did not and were unknown by Him (cf. Matt. 7:21-23).

In light of this, it would appear that it would be prudent to put any and all who claim to be spokesmen for God to a test. Just a couple of areas come to mind where a clear differentiation could become readily apparent.

The first of those areas would concern the area of salvation. We should not give an ear to those of our day who don't believe men and women need not be saved from anything. The focus of much of what passes for preaching in our day seems to be squarely on the "here and now." It is definitely true that Jesus said that one of the reasons He came to earth was "that they might have life, and that they might have it more abundantly" (John 10:10). We will consider that statement in a later chapter.

However, it is also true that He spent a considerable amount of time teaching about, and challenging people to prepare for, eternity. It would seem to me that preachers of our day would do well to follow His example in this.

Paul seems to have presented to us the proper balance between our lives on earth and our preparation for eternity when he penned, "godliness is profitable for all things, having promise of the life that now is and of that which is to come" (1 Tim. 4:8).

Is there a need for salvation? While some may deny this, Jesus and those who truly speak by His authority would emphatically say, "Yes."

Not only is the need for salvation deemphasized by many of our day, the means by which one obtains salvation is often never taught. The "sinner's prayer," the mourner's bench, the advice to "ask Jesus into your heart," and all such teachings will be found lacking when compared to God's word. Any sincere person would be well-advised to study carefully Acts 2 in order to see what was required of people on that great day. We would then need to compare what we find there with what is being taught today.

In short, the gospel remains God's power for salvation (cf. Rom. 1:16). Lifting Jesus up to a dying world remains the best "method" ever conceived (cf. John 12:32).

Also rejected out of hand should be any group that cares little, if any, about something so "mundane" as authority. Sadly, when many good people are asked today for the authority for what they believe, teach, practice, etc., they really cannot give an adequate answer. So many today have completely forgotten or chosen to ignore the admonition of the Holy Spirit in Colossians 3:17: "And whatever you do in word or deed, do all in the name of the Lord Jesus, giving thanks to God the Father through Him."

It is of more than passing interest to notice that the American Standard Version's rendering of what we have come to call "The Great Commission" states that people are to be baptized "*into* the name of the Father and of the Son and of the Holy Spirit." (Matt. 28:19, emphasis added). Since much of what Jesus and the Jewish leaders were discussing in John 5 had to do with relationship, it seems only fitting to suggest that "in the name of" can also strongly hint at our relationship with the Godhead. Volumes have been written on this subject. Much has been said and written about the Christian's relationship with his or her Father, with Christ, and with the Holy Spirit. It is not the intention here to add to all that has been said.

We would suggest that one good statement that relates to this vital subject and which should challenge each of us would be the following: "Behold what manner of love the Father has bestowed on us, that we should be called children of God! Therefore the world does not know us, because it did not know Him. Beloved, now we are children of God; and it has not yet been revealed what we shall be, but we know that when He is revealed, we shall be like Him, for we shall see Him as He is. And everyone who has this hope in Him purifies himself, just as He is pure" (1 John 3:1-3).

It is my prayer that each of us will recognize the power of the gospel, submit to the authority of Jesus, and have a relationship with Him and His Father both now and forever.

3

"I DID NOT COME TO DESTROY BUT TO FULFILL"

MATTHEW 5:17

On two different occasions, I have "preached" the "Sermon on the Mount." On both occasions, I have spent some time memorizing Jesus' words as recorded in Matthew 5-7 and have just said what He said with only two additions.

As I have begun, the first addition is that I have told those in attendance that they will hear the best sermon they will probably ever hear. I have made it clear that this is not because of who they are listening to, but because of the sermon's content. After I've said something to that effect, I try to deliver our Lord's words as found in various translations of the Bible. I use different translations for different sections of the sermon for a couple of reasons. First, I find that some translations are more accurate and/or more easily understood than some of the others in some portions of the sermon.

The second reason that I use various translations is that I really don't want those who are listening to "tune out" because they think they've heard all of this before. I want to try to make it as "fresh" to them as I can.

The only other addition I have made to the sermon is that I have extended the invitation of the Lord at the conclusion of the sermon itself. In between these two additions, those who have been in attendance have heard what those people heard so long ago. Using my normal speaking voice and style, I have been able to preach the entire sermon without comment in about the same time it usually takes me to preach any other sermon. The impact that this has is amazing. In fact, the effect is at least two-fold.

First, I am amazed. I am reminded of all that is contained in Matthew 5-7. I am challenged to the very core of my being as I read Jesus' words and try to present them to others.

Secondly, those who have been worshiping on those occasions have been amazed. Their amazement has very little to do with the fact that somebody took the time to memorize this portion of scripture. Most of them have heard preachers who can, and have, memorized much more material than that. The amazement has to do with the impact that Jesus' words has on their lives when they hear them without any sort of comment whatsoever.

There is a great deal of information in the Sermon on the Mount about attitudes and influence. One writer published a book a number of years ago with the title *The Be (Happy) Attitudes.* While there is, indeed, a great amount of material in the first twelve verses of Matthew 5 about the types of attitudes that followers of Jesus were/are to have, His discussion of attitudes is not limited to those verses.

The influence that the followers of Jesus are to have also accounts for a significant amount of material found in Matthew 5-7. When He identified His followers as "salt" and "light" in Matthew 5:13-16, He was saying much about their (our) influence. This subject is also addressed again at various places throughout the sermon.

It is at this point in the sermon that some might wonder why our Lord seemingly changes the discussion completely. After introducing the subjects of attitudes and influence, why would He then address what appears to be only a "theological point" in Matthew 5:17-20? Why introduce a discussion about the Law at this point?

It is my opinion that Jesus had not totally left the subjects of attitudes and influence in Matthew 5:17-20. Some material in this chapter is intended to discuss a few of the "theological" points that come to mind as we read the words of Jesus in this text. At the same time, it shall also be the purpose of this chapter to have something to say about attitudes and influence as it relates to this section of the Sermon on the Mount.

To more fully appreciate what Jesus said about the Law and the Prophets, we would need to try to put ourselves in the position of the Jewish people who first heard His words. It is difficult for us to imagine how His teaching must have affected them.

There are repeated indications that they thought that Jesus was about to "snatch away their spiritual security blanket." As far back as any of them chose to remember, the Law of Moses governed their lives. Admittedly, some of the teachers had perverted it with their traditions (cf. Matt. 15:6). Apparently, too, many of them saw the Law as too demanding (cf. Acts 15:10).

However, even with that being said, the Law was a constant in their lives. They were concerned about the impact that Jesus might have on what they regarded as their anchor. On various occasions, the questions that some of them asked Jesus indicates their uneasiness about Him. On more than one occasion, some of the Jews must have thought that Jesus was being much too casual at best, or totally blasphemous at worst, as He discussed the Law of Moses and/or the interpretation of that Law by the Jewish leaders of that day. There are multiple times during this sermon and elsewhere when Jesus said, "You have heard...but I say" (cf. Matt. 5:22, 28, 32, 34, 39, 42, etc.).

Most of us do not like for anybody to tamper with our comfort zone. If you disagree with that statement, try being in charge of setting the temperature on the thermostats in the building where you worship!

By the time that Jesus came to earth, many of the Jews were very comfortable with "the way things were" in their lives. As we intend to discuss in a later chapter, some of them had found comfort where there was none. Instead of following God's will for their lives, some of them had concocted a system that made them feel comfortable, even though it displeased God.

Even when all the disclaimers are considered (the Law was too strict, they concocted various ways to keep from keeping the Law, etc.), the fact remains that most of the Jews of Jesus' day were fairly comfortable. Like many of us, they had "settled in" to a lifestyle and a belief system that was comfortable for them. The actions and the teachings of our Lord did not merely tamper with their comfort level. In their view of things, His teaching was so radical that it had the potential to completely destroy their comfort level.

We wonder what their reaction would have been if Jesus had come on the scene and made this declaration, "Starting right now, everything you have ever known, believed, or done is worthless. Forget the Law of Moses and everything you've been taught about it and listen only to me!" There could be a sense in which He could have made a statement similar to that. As recorded in John 5:39, Jesus said to some Jewish leaders, "You search the Scriptures, for in them you think you have eternal life; and these are they which testify of Me."

In order to understand some of the significance of that statement and to see how it applies to our discussion here, we will look briefly at two passages of scripture. The first is found in Colossians 2:14 where the Holy Spirit inspired Paul to write that Jesus "wiped out the handwriting of requirements that was against us, which was contrary to us. And He has taken it out of the way, having nailed it to the cross."

The second passage to be considered is Luke 24:44. In this verse, Jesus said, "These are the words which I spoke to you while I was still with you, that all things must be fulfilled which were written in the Law of Moses and the Prophets and the Psalms concerning Me."

It is of interest to notice that the word "fulfilled" is in both Luke 24:44 and in Matthew 5:17. What does that word mean and how does it apply to our discussion here?

It has been observed by others that there are at least two ways to get rid of an acorn. One way would be to smash it with a hammer or in some other way totally destroy it. The other way would be to plant it in the ground, provide favorable conditions, and let it reach its potential as a mighty oak tree. This second way is what Jesus had in mind when He talked about fulfilling the law. In so many ways, the Law's potential is fulfilled in Christ. As Paul wrote in Romans 10:4, "Christ is the end of the law for righteousness to everyone who believes."

There are numerous examples of this. Many shelves on many libraries could be filled with a detailed study of this great truth and all of its implications. For example, we read of "Christ, our Passover" in 1 Corinthians 5:7. That significant event that took place centuries before Paul wrote those words and which had been seared into the minds of Jews by means of teaching and ceremony was now fulfilled in Christ. It would be interesting to study in detail how every element of the Passover all find their fulfillment in Jesus. Indeed, He is "the Lamb of God who takes away the sin of the world" (John 1:29).

Another of the many examples that could be cited centers on the significance of the role of the high priest and of the sacrifice he was to offer. It would be difficult to overstate how important this was to the Jews. Even a fairly casual study of Hebrews 8-10 will provide the student with the vitally important information that Jesus is both our high priest and that He is the sacrifice. Unlike the high priests who served during the time that the Law of Moses was in effect, He was not marred by any imperfection. Thus, He did not, as they did, need to offer sacrifice for His sins (cf. Heb. 9:7; 5:1-11).

It can also be observed that His sacrifice is superior in many ways to anything the priests who served under the Old Testament could offer. One way that this is true is that, instead of the blood of animals, it is His blood that was shed (cf. Heb. 9:12-14). It is also emphatically stated that His was a sacrifice "once for all" (Heb. 10:10). This, of course is contrasted with sacrifices "which they offer continually year by year" (Heb. 10:4).

As is the case with everything else regarding Jesus, His sacrifice is superior to anything that God had ordained to precede it. It should go without saying that it would be infinitely superior to anything mere man could ever propose or institute.

Yet another example of our Lord's fulfillment of, and superiority over, the Law can be found in a discussion of the Sabbath. No day of the week was any more important to a Jew than the Sabbath. Was it radical or just another statement about His role when Jesus asserted that He was "Lord even of the Sabbath" (Matt. 12:8)?

One of the first things that comes to the minds of many about the Sabbath is that it was a day of rest. As we think of the implications of the "great invitation" of Matthew 11:28-30, it could be argued that, not only is Jesus Lord of the Sabbath, in a sense He is the Sabbath! Before this idea is dismissed out of hand, we need to consider some of the implications of Hebrews 4:1-8. As one reads that passage, he or she is impressed with the connection between Jesus and rest.

However, before we go too far down the road of theology and doctrine, we need to also consider at least one application of all of this. Theology and doctrine are important. I pray that nothing I ever say or write will give anybody the impression that they are not. At the same time, I believe we miss a great deal if we fail to consider how all of this applies to me. All of us are struggling to find such things as identity, purpose, and fulfillment.

With that in mind, it would be helpful to suggest that, along with the Law having its fulfillment in Jesus, I have the opportunity to find my fulfillment in Him. Consider this passage from the pen of the apostle Paul: "Beware lest anyone cheat you through philosophy and empty deceit, according to the tradition of men, according to the basic principles of the world, and not according to Christ. For in Him dwells all the fullness of the Godhead bodily; and you are complete in Him, who is the head of all principality and power" (Col. 2:8-10).

Of particular interest in that passage is the word "complete." Can you guess how the Greek word translated "complete" here is translated in Matthew 5:17? It is, indeed, the same word as "fulfilled" there! It is also interesting to observe that the same word is translated "fulfilled" in Luke 24:44: "Then He said to them, 'These are the words which I spoke to you while I was still with you that all things must be fulfilled which were written in the Law of Moses and the Prophets and the Psalms concerning me.'"

To be sure, I am very thankful that I do not live under a system that was described as "a yoke ... which neither our fathers nor we were able to bear" (Acts 15:10). I am very thankful that Jesus fulfilled the Law. I am more grateful than I can express that my Lord fulfilled all that the Old Testament "pointed to" concerning Him. What a fascinating concept that is. What a blessing that is!

Even more important than all of that, I am thankful that there is a way by which I can find my fulfillment, reach my potential, and find peace in Him. I may never be a mighty oak tree, but I can try to be all that I can be for the One who gave Himself for me.

4

"THE SON OF MAN CAME EATING AND DRINKING"

MATTHEW 11:19

Some have suggested that John the Baptist had his own "Gethsemane experience." Both Matthew 11 and Luke 7 give us some information about his imprisonment. This imprisonment, of course, would result in his beheading.

It may very well be that John was already sensing the seriousness of his situation. It is not difficult to imagine that was why He "sent two of his disciples" to Jesus to ask this question: "Are You the coming One, or do we look for another?" (Matt. 11:2-3). This question led to Jesus discussing some subjects that are interesting as they apply to the setting of Jesus' earthly ministry. They are also interesting concerning how they can still apply to His followers today.

THE PROOF IS IN THE PUDDING

Many, if they had been in Jesus' position, probably would have launched into a long presentation tying together proofs from the scripture, from logic, from personal experience, and from any other source they could think of in order to answer John's disciples. It would be tempting for anybody to leave no stone unturned in order to keep John from thinking that his mission was misguided. A loving Savior would surely want a condemned man who paved the way for Him to feel good about his mission and work.

However, Jesus offered no long, detailed proof of His Deity. Rather, His answer was: "Go and tell John the things which you hear and see: The blind see and the lame walk; the lepers are cleansed and the deaf hear; the dead are raised up and the poor have the gospel preached to them. And blessed is he who is not offended because of Me" (Matt. 11:4-6).

It is almost as if Jesus was saying, "My works should convince anybody that I am everything I claim to be." This is a thread that runs through the Gospels, and especially John, that is sometimes overlooked.

We may fail to see the overarching reason for the miracles that Jesus did when we focus on the immediate situation. In other words, we may become so enamored with the wonderful deeds that met so many needs that we fail to see the "big picture." It is exciting to read about blind people being able to see, lame people who could walk, lepers who could now return to their families and friends, and even the dead being allowed to live again—all because of Jesus. Let us determine never to get so excited about these things that we fail to remember that these miracles were to establish belief in His followers then and now.

Two quotations will serve here as "bookends" in the Gospel of John to demonstrate that truth. The first of these is found in John's inspired comment concerning Jesus' first miracle: "This beginning of signs Jesus did in Cana of Galilee, and manifested His glory; and His disciples believed in Him" (John 2:11).

The second of the quotations follows John's account of the opportunity that Jesus gave Thomas to remove any doubt from his mind that Christ was, indeed, alive following His crucifixion. The next words from John's pen include all of us who read his inspired account of the ministry of Jesus: "And truly Jesus did many other signs in the presence of

His disciples, which are not written in this book; but these are written that *you may believe that Jesus is the Christ, the Son of God, and that believing you may have life in His name*" (John 20:30-31, emphasis added).

Besides being able to establish and/or fortify our faith by reading of the miracles of our Lord, what, if any, other present-day application can we make of this? Two come to mind.

First, the adage that "the proof is in the pudding" comes to mind. Those of us who wear the name of Christ need to be diligent about seeking to live our lives worthy of the name "Christian."

As I write this, I am thinking about only one example of what is a far too familiar scenario. A lady who worships where I preach talked to me about a couple she has been trying to influence for quite some time to leave the errors of the religious group they are presently a part of and embrace Christ and His church.

She and her husband and the other couple have a mutual friend who worships at another church of Christ in town. Both the "prospect" and the brother from another church share the same profession and spend quite a lot of time together. One of the big (and at this point "ungetoverable") hurdles has to do with how our brother in the Lord conducts himself at work and in social settings. His language, demeanor, and some other things may cause some souls to spend eternity separated from God --- and one of those souls could very well be his!

When members of churches of Christ admit that other religious groups are more evangelistic, have higher morals, are more generous, etc. than we are, we may be admitting more than we intend to admit. As one who has "been on the outside looking in," I can assure you that there are those who are looking for any reason to turn their back on what the Lord has to offer in His church.

It should also be remembered that Jesus gave His followers a "new commandment." Not only was this commandment to be kept, it would also serve as the identifying mark of His followers. "A new commandment I give to you, that you love one another; as I have loved you, that you also love one another. By this all will know that you are My disciples, if you have love for one another" (John 13:34-35).

Why don't we include this in those sermons we preach from time to time about the identifying marks of the church? Please do not get me wrong. I firmly believe that we need to concern ourselves with, and teach others about, the organization of the church, the worship of the church, the mission of the church, the means of entrance into the church, and other related subjects. However, our friends and neighbors need to see among us a "sincere love of the brethren" (1 Pet. 1:22). If they do not, they might not listen to anything we have to say to them about all the other subjects, as important as they are.

Before leaving this section, it is important to note that one of the things which Jesus offered as proof of His Deity required no miraculous power. It can still be done by His followers today. It can (and should) still be true today that "the poor have the gospel preached to them" (Matt. 11:5). Surely true followers of Jesus today would not "target" only people of a certain economic, educational, or social level and then assemble in a modern, state-of-the-art facility on the Lord's day to sing "The Gospel is for All."

If our "evangelistic efforts" resemble the man in Luke 14 who apparently first invited only people of his own class to a great supper, then we need to do as he later did and spend time with "the poor and the maimed and the lame and the blind" (v. 21). We also need to spend some time going "into the highways and hedges" (v. 23).

WE CAN (AND SHOULD) HAND OUT COMPLIMENTS!

What was God's plan for the kingdom? Do the terms "kingdom" and "church" refer to two totally different things? Have the prophecies concerning the kingdom been fulfilled, or are they yet to be fulfilled?

It will not be our purpose here to try to (re)answer all of those questions and many others of a similar nature. All that will be said here is that this author is not looking into the future for the fulfillment of prophecies which were fulfilled centuries ago. My understanding of the Bible gives me the assurance that, when I was baptized for the remission of my sins, I was added by the Lord to His church (cf. Acts 2:38, 47). I am also confident that I was "delivered ... from the power of darkness and translated into the kingdom of His dear Son" (Col. 1:13). If that is not true, then I presently do not have "redemption through His blood, the forgiveness of sins" (Col. 1:14).

What I propose to deal with here is something other than that. I'm wondering where some ever got the idea that Christians, congregations, and/or preachers are in competition with each other? It certainly was not from the Bible. It is interesting to notice that John and Jesus had a high regard for each other and told people about it. John had no difficulty in saying about Jesus, "It is He who, coming after me, is preferred before me, whose sandal strap I am not worthy to loose" (John 1:27). Twice in the first chapter of John's gospel, John the Baptist identified Jesus as "the Lamb of God" (vv. 29, 36). Even a casual reading of Matthew 11:7-15 will demonstrate the fact that Jesus thought highly of John and also told people of his high regard.

Present-day servants of the Lord would do well to learn this lesson. Far too many preachers spend the bulk of their time talking what another preacher is "off on." Far too many members of one congregation seem to be preoccupied with "what they're doing over there" at another congregation.

It is absolutely true that error should be exposed and dealt with. It is also absolutely true that a preoccupation with error may not be healthy. The winds of change have blown, are blowing, and will blow. We need to be aware of, and take action against, any person, doctrine, or movement that would take people away from Christ and His teaching as found in the New Testament.

However, we need also to look for the good in others. My candle does not burn brighter just because I blow yours out! The following words do not appear to be merely a suggestion: "Let no corrupt word proceed out of your mouth, but what is good for necessary edification, that it may impart grace to the hearers. And do not grieve the Holy Spirit of God, by whom you were sealed for the day of redemption. Let all bitterness, wrath, anger, clamor, and evil speaking be put away from you, with all malice. And be kind to one another, tenderhearted, forgiving one another, just as God in Christ forgave you" (Eph. 4:29-32).

All that has been written to this point has concerned the background for the actual statement that Jesus made concerning His coming. The remainder of this chapter will deal with that statement and the context in which it is found. What present-day lessons can be learned from the following words? "But to what shall I liken this generation? It is like children sitting in the marketplaces and calling to their companions, and saying 'We played the flute for you, And you did not dance; We mourned to you, And you did not lament.' For John came neither eating nor drinking, and they say, 'He has a demon.' The Son of Man came eating and drinking, and they say, 'Look, a glutton and a winebibber, a friend of tax collectors and sinners!' But wisdom is justified by her children" (Matt. 11:16-19).

The picture of the church as the body of Christ teaches that we, as Christians, complement each other (cf. Rom. 12; 1 Cor. 12). The New Testament also teaches that we should express compliments to each other.

GOD'S SERVANTS ARE DIFFERENT

We readily accept the fact that the Bible teaches that Christians are to be different from the world. Whether we comply with that teaching may be material for another discussion. 2 Corinthians 6:14-18 is just one passage that demonstrates we are to "come out" of the sinful things of the world. We cannot talk like the lost, dress like the lost, have the same habits as the lost and, at the same time, be the "salt of the earth" and "the light of the world" (Matt. 5:13-14).

The point of the discussion here is not about our relationship (or lack thereof) with the world. It is about our relationship with one another. We can be different from one another and still be Christians! Jesus and John the Baptist had different diets, personalities, and methods, but each one fulfilled God's plan for His ministry. That same thing can be true with us!

Interestingly enough, when Jesus chose His twelve apostles, He did not choose one and then clone eleven more. There were "white collar" and "blue collar" apostles. There was one who had "worked for the government" and one who apparently would have overthrown the government by force if given the chance.

It could be argued that the only time when all of the members of the church could possibly have been all alike might have been on Pentecost. It doesn't take long to realize that such was not even the case then. People from a variety of different places and who spoke different languages and dialects were joined in their allegiance to Christ. It is worth noting that they were "added to" those who had actually spent time with Jesus and had already been His followers.

There has never been a time when all of the followers of Jesus looked alike, sounded alike, talked alike, or were in any other way alike—except for their allegiance to Him and His teaching. It needs to be remembered that we are His body and while we cannot all have the same function, each of us has an important function (cf. 1 Cor. 12:12ff).

NO MATTER WHAT YOU DO, SOMEBODY WILL BE THERE TO CRITICIZE

The people of Jesus' day were like children who couldn't be satisfied "playing parade" or "playing funeral" (cf. Matt. 11:16-17). Their ancestors griped and complained about the food God provided for them, the leadership God provided for them, and a host of other things. They fit in well with those who were critical of the woman who broke the alabaster box and anointed Jesus with the fragrant oil it contained (cf. Mark 14:1-9). We need to remember that Jesus' desire was that a part of this account should be preached wherever the gospel is preached. It was not the criticism, but her selfless act of service that He commended and wanted to be preached.

Another example of unjust criticism is to be found in Matthew 19. It would be easy to imagine why the disciples of our Lord would be upset with what they considered to be an untimely interruption. After all, He was teaching them something about an extremely important and sensitive subject. Right in the middle of the discussion about marriage, divorce, and remarriage some young children are brought to Jesus. His disciples were critical of those who brought the children, but Jesus rebuked the disciples.

Before we are tempted to join the rank of the critics, it might be good to remember that it is difficult, if not impossible, to find a monument that honors a critic. Monuments are built to honor doers, not complainers.

Maybe, too, the following quotation will be helpful as we try to defeat criticism in our own minds. Somebody has observed that, "Criticism is something you can avoid by saying nothing, doing nothing and being nothing." Another person asked, "How often have you met a critic of the church who tried to make it better?"

It seems that there are people like Goldilocks in the modern church. The environment must be just right; they have no trouble expressing displeasure when it is not; when they find a place that fits their "comfort level," they curl up and go to sleep!

AS ALWAYS, WE CAN LEARN MUCH FROM THE EXAMPLE OF JESUS

Four things are indicated about our Lord in Matthew 11 that need to be studied and imitated by His followers. First, there is every indication here and elsewhere that Jesus was a social person. Repeatedly in the record we have of His earthly ministry, we find Him at banquets (sometimes as the guest of honor), invited into peoples' homes, talking to a small or large group of people, and in other environments where people were enjoying some time together.

One of the "balancing acts" that preachers (and others) find themselves performing is in trying to find the correct ratio between time and energy spent in solitude studying God's word and time and energy spent "socializing." Great congregations are not built solely in a preacher's study and great sermons are not built on a golf course or at a ballgame.

Along with this, it is apparent as we read the New Testament that Jesus was approachable. People from every station and walk in life seemed to have felt comfortable spending time with Him and talking to Him. Apparently, His demeanor did not "put people off." As Christians, we need to ask ourselves if people feel comfortable being around us and/or talking to us.

Some of those who talked to Jesus were not where they should have been morally, religiously, or in other ways. Jesus never compromised what was right in any area. At the same time, His personality was such that people who desperately needed to hear His message were given that opportunity. We could do no better than to treat people the same way.

Along with this, it appears that Jesus was enjoyable to be around. This may be just another way of saying that He was approachable, but it also may be saying something about His impact on a gathering of people. He saw every occasion as an occasion to reach out to others and often to use those occasions as opportunities to teach.

His condemnation of sin and religious error did not sour His disposition. His followers today need to ask ourselves if a room brightens when we enter it—or does it get brighter when we leave?

Finally, it must not be overlooked that Jesus was still focused on a very serious mission. In Matthew 11:20-30, a discussion of the judgment is found along with what is sometimes called "The Great Invitation" of verses 28-30.

Eternity was always in the mind of Jesus. The fact that there is going to be a judgment colored everything He did. The desire for people to find the rest that is available in Him was strong.

We have not fulfilled our mission in the twenty-first century or any other century if we merely are amiable, pleasant, and social people. People need to be taught the gospel and persuaded to obey it.

God's wisdom is not defeated or frustrated by those who think of themselves as wise in the manner in which the world views wisdom (cf. 1 Cor. 1:18-21). God's wisdom is demonstrated in lives that are changed. Truly, "wisdom is justified by her children" (Matt. 11:19).

5

"THINK NOT THAT I CAME TO SEND PEACE ON EARTH: I CAME NOT TO SEND PEACE, BUT A SWORD"

MATTHEW 10:34

"DO YOU SUPPOSE THAT I CAME TO GIVE PEACE ON EARTH? I TELL YOU, NOT AT ALL, BUT RATHER DIVISION"

LUKE 12:51

The two statements reproduced above are similar in many very apparent ways. At the same time, the two statements were made on two different occasions under two different sets of circumstances. These differences will play a part in our discussion later and will, hopefully, help us to better understand them and make an application for us today.

First, we need to deal with what looks, at first glance, like a major discrepancy between what these two statements say and what is said elsewhere. Did not Isaiah prophesy that He would be known as the

"Prince of Peace" (Isa. 9:6)? What did Zacharias mean when he spoke of his son, John the Baptist, being the one who would "guide our feet into the way of peace" (Luke 1:79) if he was not talking about pointing people to Jesus? Why would the angels announce the birth of Jesus by saying, in part, "peace, goodwill toward men" (Luke 2:14)? Why did the subject of peace come up in Jesus' discussion recorded in John 14-16 with the apostles?

> Peace I leave with you, My peace I give to you; not as the world gives do I give to you. Let not your heart be troubled, neither let it be afraid.
>
> John 14:27

> These things I have spoken to you, that in Me you may have peace. In the world you will have tribulation; but be of good cheer, I have overcome the world.
>
> John 16:33

It is very interesting that the subject of peace also was included in this statement made to His apostles after His resurrection: "Peace to you! As the Father has sent Me, I also send you" (John 20:21).

It seems to be very evident that our Lord lived in a hostile environment. This may very well have played a major role in His statements to His followers about peace. There is abundant evidence that He told them they were also part of a hostile environment and that they did, in fact, experience criticism, ridicule, and, in some cases, physical violence and death because of their allegiance to Him.

What we all too often forget, overlook, or try to ignore is that the followers of Jesus in our present time also live in a hostile environment. While our faith does not put our lives in jeopardy in our society (at least not yet), we need to be aware of a couple of truths.

First, there are societies, even in our day and time, where people suffer in much the same way as did followers of Christ in the first century and for the same reason. Alienation, preferential treatment, and even physical violence and death are the prices paid by some of our brothers and sisters in some parts of the world. Not all of the Christians in the world are in the United States!

Secondly, those of us who are Christians in the United States are living in a society that is becoming increasingly hostile to our Lord and His teaching. One would have to be almost out of touch with reality to not realize that the most ungodly people and ideas are being increasingly promoted and celebrated in our nation, while the teachings of Christ and the followers of Christ are being increasingly relegated to a "second-class" status. We may still find religious slogans and symbols on some of our currency and public structures, but the teachings of our Lord and those who wear His name are under attack.

At this time, the attacks are mostly in the intellectual, social, political, legal, and moral realms. How much longer could it be before we suffer in the same way and to the same extent as the first-century Christians? How much longer could it be before we need to hear our Savior's words about peace? Could it be that we need to consider them now?

Much can be learned from a consideration of the two statements from the lips of our Lord with which we began this chapter as we consider them in the order in which Jesus said them. According to *The Fourfold Gospel* by J. W. McGarvey and Philip Y. Pendleton, the statement from Luke's gospel was spoken before the statement in Matthew's gospel. Some consideration will be given here to some implications of that.

The background of the statement in Luke is interesting. This is especially true when we consider the people to whom Jesus made the various statements in Luke 12. According to Luke 12:1, there was "an innumerable multitude of people [who] had gathered together" Interestingly, though, that same verse informs us that the material found through verse 12 was spoken "to his disciples first of all" Verse 13 records an interruption in Jesus' teaching when "one from the crowd" asked

Him a question. After quickly dealing with that question, Jesus "spoke a parable to them" (v. 16). We might safely assume that the next few verses were meant for the entire multitude because of the phrase recorded a few verses later, where we are informed that His attention shifted to "His disciples" (v. 22).

An interesting question is asked by Peter in verse 41: "Lord do You speak this parable only to us or to all people?" Jesus' answer to that question in verses 42-48 forms the immediate backdrop for the text we are considering. His answer indicates strongly that this portion of His teaching was intended primarily for His chosen ones, but that the teaching also had implications for a much wider audience (including us).

It is in this context that we find the passage from which our verse under consideration is found. In its immediate context, we read the following:

> I came to send fire on the earth, and how I wish it were already kindled! But I have a baptism to be baptized with, and how distressed I am till it is accomplished! Do you suppose that I came to give peace on earth? I tell you, not at all, but rather division. For from now on five in one house will be divided: three against two, and two against three. Father will be divided against son and son against father, mother against daughter and daughter against mother, mother-in-law against her daughter-in-law and daughter-in-law against her mother-in-law.
>
> Luke 12:49-53

The next time (chronologically) we find words very similar to these is in Matthew 10. But in this context, Jesus had chosen twelve of His disciples as apostles (Luke 6:13) and was sending them on what we have come to know as the "limited commission." A reading of His instructions to them demonstrates clearly that He was alerting them to the dangers they would face. Among those things He wanted them to be aware of was that "men ... will deliver you up to councils and scourge you in their synagogues" (v. 17); that they would "be hated by all for My name's sake" (v. 22); and that they would be persecuted (cf. v. 23).

The account in John 20:21 where peace is mentioned is also connected to our Lord sending His apostles on a mission. It appears that He was preparing them for the time when they would, indeed, carry out the Great Commission when He said to them, "Peace to you! As the Father has sent Me, I also send you."

Notice a "progression" in treatment and opinion that took place during our Lord's earthly ministry. First, He compared people of His day (especially the Jews) to children who could not be satisfied. In the last chapter, we have already considered some of this material that is found in Matthew 11 and Luke 7.

In the texts we have just considered, the subject moves far beyond mere criticism. In Luke's account, Jesus' message is compared to a fire that ultimately led to His crucifixion. In the record found in Matthew 10, He makes it clear to His apostles that, while carrying out the "limited commission," they would be met by open, violent opposition.

Although opposition is not mentioned in John 20:21, we should have no trouble believing that the apostles fully expected to deal with such as they carried out the Great Commission. After all, Jesus had already told them to expect this kind of treatment: "They will put you out of the synagogues; yes, the time is coming that whoever kills you will think that he offers God service" (John 16:2).

What kind of peace can there be in a hostile environment? What kind of peace is there when a person is hated to the point that even his or her own family members become enemies?

These are questions people of the first century needed to have answered. These are questions people of the twenty-first century need answers to as well. That "divisive" message of Jesus means several things. Some of them will be discussed here.

I CAN KNOW THAT PEACE DOES NOT ALWAYS MEAN THE ABSENCE OF CONFLICT.

All too often, we assume that the peace the Bible talks about and the peace for which some are still desperately searching means that everything in our lives is to be running smoothly. If there are any bumps in the road, some cannot seriously contemplate there being any peace.

There is a problem with that kind of thinking. Nobody goes through life without problems, challenges, opposition, illness, and/or setbacks of one kind or another. Most of us cannot imagine all that the apostle Paul went through. Yet He was the one who wrote about "the peace of God which surpasses all understanding" (Phil. 4:7).

Paul's writing and experiences inform us that peace is possible in the middle of trials, temptations, opposition, etc. Somebody long ago tried to explain the peace Christ gives us by describing an assignment given to two painters. They were trying to depict that peace in a painting.

The first painter produced a beautiful scene. The sun was shining, birds appeared as though they were floating through the air, the sky was blue, animals of the field were pictured as grazing contentedly on rolling pastures, etc. In short, everything appeared peaceful, serene, perfect.

The second painter produced an entirely different picture. A violent storm darkened the sky. Lightning bolts broke through the darkness. Rain poured down a steep rock cliff. There was one small ledge on that rock cliff. On that ledge, there was a mother eagle protecting her little ones.

Which picture is your concept of biblical peace? If you chose the first, I invite you to look again at some of the great heroes of faith in the Bible and in your own life.

I CAN KNOW THE DIFFERENCE BETWEEN JOY AND PLEASURE.

A lot of what is so unsettling to so many people is the constant quest for pleasure, happiness, or what they think is joy. Lives are in turmoil and know absolutely no peace because they are searching for something that is not there.

How many people do you know who have tried a lot of what the world has to offer that is supposed to make a person feel fulfilled? How many do you know well enough to know if they are truly happy? I am thinking of one man I know who, by the standards of the world, "has it made." Why then did he say with tears running down his cheeks, "I just want to be happy!"?

It took me a while to notice something very important that is taught in the eleventh chapter of Hebrews. For a long time, I thought that "religious types" were telling me that sin is not fun. I looked around at some who were practicing sins of various kinds, and while they may not have been fulfilled, it did look to me like they were having fun; at least at times.

One day, the words of Hebrews 11:25 finally made an impact on me. The writer of Hebrews informs us about the "pleasures of sin" that Moses gave up! We probably need to repent immediately if we have been trying to teach our young people, or people of any age, that sin is not fun. We need to be honest with them and with ourselves and admit that sin can be enjoyable—at least temporarily.

However, we need, at the same time, to make sure they and we understand the vast difference between fun or pleasure on the one hand and peace and true joy on the other. There is a world of difference. No, there is an eternity of difference!

I CAN KNOW THAT THE SMALLEST ACT OF SERVICE DOES NOT GO UNNOTICED.

There is an interesting "follow-up" in Matthew's account of our Lord's statement about the division that His teaching would cause. To be sure, He is speaking to those twelve apostles He was sending on the "limited commission," but there are still present-day applications of these words:

"He who receives you receives Me, and he who receives Me receives Him who sent Me. He who receives a prophet in the name of a prophet shall receive a prophet's reward. And he who receives a righteous man in the name of a righteous man shall receive a righteous man's reward. And whoever gives one of these little ones only a cup of cold water in the name of a disciple, assuredly, I say to you, he shall by no means lose his reward" (Matt. 10:40-42).

What a comfort it is to know that the same Lord who noticed the poor widow as she cast in her two mites (cf. Matt. 12:41-44) and who said complimentary things about those who would provide "only a cup of cold water" can also see my feeble attempts to serve Him.

It seems that, all too often, people are mistaken about which members are the real "backbone" of a given congregation. It has been my observation that many quickly look to those in "leadership positions" as the ones who fill this role. Sometimes a more careful observation (or more time with a particular congregation) will reveal a much different picture. Very often, it is those who work beyond the reach of the spotlight and whose names do not appear regularly in the bulletin who are the real reasons why a particular congregation can accomplish what it is accomplishing for the Lord.

I find the story of Dorcas, as recorded in Acts 9, to be fascinating. Though she held no "official position" and "just" made tunics and garments, the church at Joppa thought so highly of her that, when she died, they sent for Peter. The text does not record what they thought Peter could do, but it does record that, when her life was restored, "it became known throughout all Joppa" (Acts 9:42).

We need to consider the vast difference in how two men are described in 3 John. In verses 9-10, we are introduced to Diotrephes. He is described as one who "loves to have the preeminence" (v. 9) and used "malicious words" against John and others (v. 10). That same verse informs us that he decided who should and who should not be accepted into the church's fellowship.

In verse 12 of that same epistle, we are introduced to a man we know very little about. All we know is that "Demetrius has a good testimony from all, and from the truth itself..."

What a contrast!

All we know about these two men is recorded here. For all time and into eternity, one will be known for his boastful, arrogant, self-promotion. The other man may have worked in the shadows, but his work was noticed by the One who will judge all of us.

Among the other things taught in 1 Corinthians 12 and Romans 12 is that there are no unimportant members of the body of Christ. Each of us is important to our Lord and each act of service (even the "menial" ones) will be rewarded.

I CAN KNOW WHO MY FATHER IS.

I still remember clearly, though it has been years ago, how I felt when my children were very small. I knew that, if something tragic happened, and they did not live beyond the age of two or three, their memory would be a part of my life until I drew my last breath. As long as I could remember anything, I would remember my precious children.

At the same time, the realization struck me that, if the tables were turned and I was the one who departed this life during that same time, I would only be a man they saw in some old photographs. They would go through life never remembering me and never knowing me. There might be something unsettling about that. People who never knew their fathers may, at times, have questions and concerns that bother them in various ways.

Sadly, many people living today do not know who their heavenly Father is. There is a longing; there are questions; there is an emptiness. There is no real peace because these people do not know who they really are and do not know the One who has made it possible for them to be His children.

Both the birth process and the adoption process are used in the New

Testament to describe how we become members of God's great family. We will not, at this time, explore all of the scriptures dealing with this or describe in detail the process. Our purpose here is to try to make the point that any question about my "heritage" can be answered by the Bible. Specifically, I can rest in the assurance of knowing who my Father is. It doesn't stop there. He does not want me just to know about Him; He calls us to know Him.

Consider, for example, this challenging and comforting statement our Lord made in the early part of His prayer to His Father prior to the cross: "And this is eternal life, that they may know You, the only true God, and Jesus Christ whom You have sent" (John 17:3). Space will not allow us to explore all of the implications of that one sentence, but it is very apparent that one great purpose of our Lord's mission and message is that we might not just know about God, but that we might come to know God as our Father. The implications of this would fill volumes. Only a very few will be mentioned here.

- My Father wants what is best for me (cf. Matt. 7:7-11).
- My Father wants a close relationship with me. This is typified in Jesus' lament over Jerusalem (Matt. 23:37).
- My Father will discipline me (cf. Heb. 12:3-11).
- My Father will accept me back when I have truly repented of sin in my life (cf. Luke 15:11-32).
- My Father can wipe away my tears (cf. Rev. 21:4).

I CAN KNOW WHERE MY REAL FAMILY IS.

For four and a half years, my wife and I really did not have a church family. We were spending almost every Sunday morning, Sunday evening, and Wednesday evening at a different congregation. We had a "home congregation," but about all we were able to contribute to its work was in the form of our monetary support. The nature of our work in promoting Christian education kept us away from them most of the time.

We learned a lot during those years. One of the things we learned was that we are a part of a large and wonderful family. We were meeting family members who were new to us. These wonderful brothers and sisters made us feel "right at home." The concept of "the whole family in heaven and earth" (Eph. 3:15) took on a new meaning for us.

I truly feel sorry for people who do not understand what a blessing it is to be a part of the greatest family there ever has been or ever will be. We have already discussed briefly the idea that God is our Father, but what about the truth that Jesus is my older brother?

One of the most sobering and challenging verses in the New Testament is found in Hebrews 2:11, "For both He who sanctifies and those who are being sanctified are all of one, for which reason He is not ashamed to call them brethren." To think that the sinless, eternal, powerful Son of God is not ashamed of me as a brother is something I cannot fully comprehend.

Added to that great truth is the fact that I have brothers and sisters I have yet to meet. Have you ever had the experience of meeting somebody for the first time and realizing that "there's just something" about that person, only to find out after some conversation that he or she is your brother or sister in Christ? Isn't that a thrilling experience?

However, as thrilling and satisfying as that is, we need never to lose sight of the value of a home congregation and the valuable relationships available there. While my wife and I were meeting all sorts of wonderful people during those "disconnected years," we desperately longed for the feelings of belonging, acceptance, support, encouragement, and identity that comes only by being an active part of the Lord's work in a local setting.

Both of my parents passed away during the time we were traveling so much. We happened to be in town when each of them passed from this life. In fact, I was at my father's bedside when he drew his last breath. People reached out to us in so many ways. We can never repay people for all of the kindness demonstrated to us during those difficult times. At the same time, I cannot help but believe that these times would have been much easier if we could have leaned on those with whom we worshiped on a regular basis and with whom we worked side by side on a regular basis. The song "God's Family" takes on an entirely new meaning when you don't have one that you feel really close to in a local setting.

I CAN KNOW WHAT MY DESTINY IS.

Some have made the observation that God is in the "separating business." That process began when He separated light from dark (cf. Gen. 1:4) and will continue until He separates "those who have done good to the resurrection of life [from] those who have done evil to the resurrection of condemnation" (John 5:29).

Uncertainty is a major hindrance to peace of mind. We feel very uncomfortable with the unknown in almost any area of our lives. For example, not knowing the type and/or severity of a physical problem is often more difficult to deal with than receiving unfavorable news.

In a somewhat similar manner, there are those who are so calloused that they know and understand they are destined to spend eternity apart from everything good and holy, but they do not care. Some even seem to glory in the ungodly lives they live and the destiny they face.

Sadly, for some, the only other alternative is to "hope" that they make it to heaven. They hear and read about peace, but it is a foreign concept to them. Their entire lives are spent under a cloud of doubt.

Maybe some of this type of thinking is a reaction to those who have not met God's conditions of pardon as laid out in the New Testament, but who, at the same time, boast of their relationship with God and their assurance of eternal salvation. Some of us may be hesitant to express confidence about our destiny because of the unfounded confidence of these individuals.

Possibly we need to re-read and seriously consider the inspired words of 1 John 5:13: "These things I have written to you who believe in the name of the Son of God, that you may know that you have eternal life, and that you may continue to believe in the name of the Son of God."

We cannot be among those who cry, "Peace. peace; when there is no peace" (Jer. 6:14; 8:11). We can, however, heed Paul's instructions in Philippians 4:9, "The things which you learned and received and heard and saw in me, do, and the God of peace will be with you."

6

"I DID NOT COME TO CALL THE RIGHTEOUS, BUT SINNERS, TO REPENTANCE"

MATTHEW 9:13

While the background of each of the statements we are considering, may vary in many aspects (time, location, audience, etc.), there seems to be one constant. It seems that the reader can almost expect some group of the Jewish leaders to be critical. Even a casual reader of the gospels is not surprised to find these people critical of somebody for something. If they are not found to be critical of Jesus, Himself, they are found being critical of His followers and/or those who are in His company to learn, asking for some sort of help from Him, or for some other reason.

The events surrounding the statement found recorded in Matthew 9:13, Mark 2:17, and Luke 6:32 are certainly no exception to that. In the immediate context, Jesus had invited Matthew (Levi) to leave his job of collecting taxes and to follow Him. It seems that not much time elapsed between this event and the event that caused the Pharisees to be very critical (again).

According to Luke's account, "Levi gave Him a great feast in his own house. And there were a great number of tax collectors and others who sat down with them" (5:29). Matthew and Mark identify these "others" as "sinners" (Matt. 9:10; Mark 15). Therein rested the problem. The scribes and the Pharisees questioned Jesus' disciples about His association with these sorts of people.

All three synoptic gospels record some form of the statement reproduced below as at least part of our Lord's answer. Jesus' statement, as recorded in both Mark's account and Luke's account, states that Jesus said: "Those who are well have no need of a physician, but those who are sick. I have not come to call the righteous, but sinners, to repentance" (Mark 2:17; Luke 5:32).

However, Matthew adds some additional information. According to him, Jesus said, "Those who are well have no need of a physician, but those who are sick. But go and learn what this means: 'I desire mercy and not sacrifice.' For I did not come to call the righteous, but sinners, to repentance." This is not the first time we find the phrase "I desire mercy and not sacrifice" in God's Word. Hosea was inspired to write those same words in Hosea 6:6. It is of more than casual interest that, in the same verse, he connected that thought with "and the knowledge of God more than burnt offerings."

In the context of Hosea's writing, we find some other matters of interest. Among God's complaints against His people in Hosea 6 were the following: God's people were transgressing His covenant; their priests were committing horrible acts; gross immorality was being practiced (cf. vv. 7, 9-10).

This thought is also found in another place in the gospels. In Matthew 12:7, it is found in the form of a "challenge" to the Pharisees.

In this instance, the Pharisees were critical (yet again) about something they determined to be a violation of the Sabbath by the disciples of Jesus. On this particular Sabbath day, the disciples were passing through a field of grain. Also on this particular day, they "were hungry, and began to pluck heads of grain and to eat" (v. 1). It is not our purpose here to explore our Lord's entire answer to the Pharisees on this occasion. For the purpose of our study in this chapter, though, it is important to notice that He said to the Pharisees, "But if you had known what this means, 'I desire mercy and not sacrifice' you would not have condemned the guiltless" (Matt. 12:7).

How ironic this is! The very ones who considered themselves to be the real experts on the Law and the Prophets were being challenged concerning their knowledge and/or understanding of the same! Did they not consider themselves to be righteous? Were they, in actuality, righteous in God's sight? Did Jesus' statement about not coming to call the righteous mean that they did not need to be called or that they were left out of His call? These are at least some of the questions we will explore in the remainder of this chapter.

The concept of righteousness can be a slippery one to grasp at times. The same Bible that informs us that "there is none righteous, no not one" (Rom. 3:10) also informs us about people who were considered to be righteous. One interesting example of this is found in Matthew 23:35 where Abel is referred to as "righteous Abel." It is of more than passing interest also to consider these words of Jesus to His disciples as recorded in Matthew 13:17—"I say to you that many prophets and righteous men desired to see what you see, and did not see it, and to hear what you hear, and did not hear it."

Apparently, according to these two passages and others, there is a sense in which people living before the time of Christ could be considered righteous. It is suggested here that an explanation of that can be found in the two Psalms which are quoted by Paul in Romans 3:10. Instead of asserting that "there is none righteous" (Rom. 3:10), both Psalm 14:3 and Psalm 53:3 state that "there is none who does good."

There is a sense, then, that people of all ages could be deemed as righteous. This may help to explain the following description of the parents of John the Baptist. In Luke 1:6, this glowing description of Zacharias and Elizabeth is found: "And they were both righteous before God, walking in all the commandments and ordinances of the Lord blameless."

We are well aware of the truth that "Christ is the end of the law for righteousness to every one that believeth" (Rom. 10:4). Nothing that has been written in the preceding paragraph(s) is meant to suggest otherwise. All that is suggested is that which is stated in Romans 1:17: "For in it the righteousness of God is revealed from faith to faith; as it is written, 'The just shall live by faith.'" The verse immediately before verse 17 informs the reader that the "it" of verse 17 is "the gospel."

Notice the quotation cited at the end of verse 17. Where "it is written" is in Habakkuk 2:4. A careful consideration of that verse may move us closer to a fuller understanding of what Jesus meant in the text(s) we are considering in this chapter. The quotation in Habakkuk is: "Behold the proud, His soul is not upright in him; But the just shall live by his faith."

It is important to notice two things about this verse. First, Habakkuk informs us that the just shall live by his faith. Faith is a very personal and individual matter. There is, indeed, a "system" of faith to which followers of Christ must adhere in order to be pleasing to Him (cf. Jude 3). At the same time, my responsibility to do that is just that; my responsibility.

Since the same Greek word is translated both "just" and "righteous" in the New Testament, it does not seem to do any injustice to the meaning of Habakkuk 2:4 to state that the righteous shall live by his faith. In fact, the word "righteous" is used in the following translations of Habakkuk 2:4: ASV, NASV, RSV, ESV, and NIV.

Another interesting aspect of Habakkuk 2:4 is that two distinct individuals (or types of individuals) are described. "The just (who) shall live by his faith" is contrasted with "the proud (whose) soul is not upright in him."

Who were those Jesus condemned most often for their arrogance and pride? Was it not the same scribes and Pharisees to whom He addressed the remarks we began discussing at the beginning of this chapter?

Take the time to read through our Lord's denunciation of these people as found in Matthew 23. Though the word "pride" is not used, it is very apparent that they had a problem with that.

It is also very apparent that they did not think they had a problem with that, or with anything else for that matter. In the vernacular of some of our day, they thought they "had it all together." In the words of Jesus, they "outwardly appear[ed] righteous to men" (v. 28). They even "adorn[ed] the monuments of the righteous" (v. 29).

Think of that for a minute. They appeared to be righteous, but they were not. Besides that, they were paying homage to a group they thought they were a part of, but from which they were, in fact, excluded. They couldn't "see" what they really were.

Verse 23 is a key verse in this entire discussion: "Woe to you, scribes and Pharisees, hypocrites! For you pay tithe of mint and anise and cummin, and have neglected the weightier matters of the law: justice and mercy and faith. These you ought to have done, without leaving the others undone." At least two things are worthy of noting here. First, they had the "form" right, but the "function" was far from right. Religious ceremony was being meticulously observed, but the reason for its observance and the impact made on their treatment of others was sorely lacking.

Secondly, one of the omissions of which they were guilty was "mercy." This is, of course, the same word and concept we have looked at earlier where Jesus challenged the Pharisees about something they should have already known and practiced (cf. Matt. 9:13, 12:7).

It seems that part of their problem (and what could become part of our problem) has to do with how our belief system and/or our religious practice has an effect on our relationship with God and the treatment of our fellow man. It can become far too easy to "construct" a system that is built on a very faulty foundation. That type of system or practice makes me feel good, but it offers me nothing in terms of a proper relationship with God.

Is this not at least part of the meaning of Romans 10:1-3? "Brethren, my heart's desire and prayer to God for Israel is that they may be saved. For I bear them witness that they have a zeal for God, but not according to knowledge. For they being ignorant of God's righteousness, and seeking to establish their own righteousness, have not submitted to the righteousness of God."

Were the people about whom Paul was writing truly righteous? The answer to that question depends entirely upon perspective. From their perspective (like the perspective of the Pharisees of Jesus' day and like what could be my perspective) the answer was a resounding, "Yes!"

However, a sobering description of some people of Jesus' day was that they "trusted in themselves that they were righteous, and despised others" (Luke 18:9). The verse in which that description is found informs us that these were the people to whom Jesus spoke a parable. It is extremely interesting to notice that the parable which follows is the one that begins with these words: "Two men went up to the temple to pray, one a Pharisee and the other a tax collector" (Luke 18:10).

This very familiar parable points out the vast difference between the smugly self-righteous Pharisee and the humble, self-deprecating tax collector. Those who truly want to please God cannot afford to forget the application Jesus made of this parable. Speaking of the tax collector and making the application, He said, "I tell you, this man went down to his house justified rather than the other; for everyone who exalts himself will be humbled, and he who humbles himself will be exalted" (Luke 18:14).

If "all have sinned and fall short of the glory of God," (Rom. 3:23) and if we are "called by [the] gospel" (2 Thess. 2:14), and if the gospel is to be preached to "every creature" (Mark 16:15), then who are the "righteous" whom Jesus did not come to call? It seems that the answer to that would be those during His time on earth and in every age who had (have) no awareness of their need for His message. In yet another confrontation with the scribes and Pharisees, Jesus referred to them in this manner: "They are blind leaders of the blind" (Matt. 15:24). In that same verse, He said, "Let them alone… And if the blind leads the blind, both will fall into the ditch."

Awareness, then, seems to be important in understanding who these "righteous" people were to whom Jesus was referring. Before any change can be made on any level, there must first be an awareness of a need to change. Awareness, by itself, does not completely take care of the issue. We must remember that Jesus came to "call...the sinners to repentance" (Luke 5:32).

Repentance is a foreign concept to many, but it is a vital part of what the people on the day of Pentecost were told to do (cf. Acts 2:38). Repentance is a command for all people (cf. Acts 17:30). All who would seek to please God will see the need for, and will carry out the command to, repent.

As long as one is sailing through life without giving any thought to things of eternal importance, he or she will feel no compunction to repent. The wonderful message of the gospel will have no appeal for a person like this. However, those who think of the real purpose of life will hear the call of the gospel and will answer the challenge to repent. They will not merely reform. Neither will they merely be sorry. Even godly sorrow can only lead to repentance. It is not, itself, repentance (cf. 2 Cor. 7:8-10). Repentance is much more radical than either reformation or sorrow --- or even remorse.

Brother Hugo McCord's translation of the New Testament has "change of heart" for repentance. A contemporary translation called "God's Word" has this interesting rendering of the concept of repentance: "Turn to God and change the way you think and act."

Since all of us are sinners, all of us are in need of repentance. Those who in the language of Jesus when He explained the Parable of the Sower, have "a noble and good heart" (Luke 8:15), will, according to Him, "accept [the word] and bear fruit" (Mark 4:20). The gospel of Christ has a great appeal for them.

Sadly, however, there are those whose hearts are described by the other types of ground in this parable. The most glorious message the world has ever known will bear no lasting fruit in their lives. "Let them alone." Please allow those words to sink deeply into your consciousness. There were people of Jesus' day who, because of their arrogance, self-righteousness, callousness, and indifference, would not benefit at all from time spent with Jesus or His followers.

Sadly, that is not the last time we find words to that effect. Notice what Paul and Barnabas said to some of the leaders of the Jews of their day in Acts 13:46: "It was necessary that the word of God should be spoken to you first; but since you reject it, and judge yourselves unworthy of everlasting life, behold, we turn to the Gentiles."

Surely no blindness is as terrible as spiritual blindness. What a tragedy it is to have no sense of direction or purpose in life. How sad that some can "see" no need to hear and obey the gospel of Christ.

For some, the problem is described in 2 Corinthians 4:3-4: "But if our gospel be hid, it is hid to them that are lost: In whom the god of this world hath blinded the minds of them which believe not, lest the light of the glorious gospel of Christ, who is the image of God, should shine unto them. What a sad commentary on so many even of our day and time. They are so caught up in what the world has to offer that the gospel has absolutely no appeal to them."

Another sad thought is that Christians can also become blinded. After detailing and discussing briefly the importance of what we have come to know as the "Christian graces" in 2 Peter 1:5-8, Peter then adds this comment in verse 9: "For he who lacks these things is shortsighted, even to blindness, and has forgotten that he was cleansed from his old sins."

Paul's self-description in Philippians 3 is enlightening. He had been one of the Pharisees (v. 5). He wrote this about his former life as a Pharisee, "concerning the righteousness which is in the law, blameless" (v. 6). However, more than mere physical sight was restored to him in Damascus. This is seen by the following:

> But what things were gain to me, these I have counted loss for Christ. Yet indeed I also count all things loss for the excellence of the knowledge of Christ Jesus my Lord, for whom I have suffered the loss of all things, and count them as rubbish, that I may gain Christ and be found in Him, not having my own righteousness, which

> is from the law, but that which is through faith in Christ, the righteousness which is from God by faith; that I may know Him and the power of His resurrection, and the fellowship of His sufferings, being conformed to His death, if, by any means, I may attain to the resurrection from the dead.
>
> Philippians 3:7-11

Both Paul and those who continue to read his words can be eternally thankful for the fact that he finally "saw" what really mattered. Once he was able to do that, he spent the remainder of his life getting others to come to that same understanding. We would do well to follow his example in this.

There have been, and there always will be, those who will reject God's saving message. One does not have to be what some would label as "the chiefest of sinners" for this to be true. Some will do so and will forfeit their soul due to their inflated and misguided sense of (self)-righteousness. Through the gospel, Jesus is still calling (cf. 2 Thess. 2:14).

Are you listening? Am I?

7

"FOR THE SON OF MAN HAS COME TO SAVE THAT WHICH WAS LOST"

MATTHEW 18:11

It was one of those nice days that little boys dearly love. On this particular day, this little boy was playing outside and was in his own little world. The gravel road was the "uncrossable barrier." Under no circumstances was he allowed to cross that road.

Usually, he did not get anywhere near that road. Big cars went by at what seemed to a little boy a very, very fast speed. Besides that, there really was nothing on the other side that looked too appealing; just an open field that one of the men down the road farmed. Even farther in the distance, there was an area that was heavily wooded and grown up with weeds, bushes, and who knows what else.

The circumstances on this day were not normal, however. A dog was involved. Anybody who knows anything about boys and dogs knows that circumstances are never normal when one finds that combination.

The little boy played and played with the dog. It was fun to pet him, wrestle with him, and chase him all around the yard. The boy never really noticed when the "uncrossable barrier" was, in fact, crossed. All he was aware of was that he was having fun with the dog.

Well, that's not really all he was aware of. He became aware of the fact that he was in an open field and then in a wooded area he had never been in before, but he was too preoccupied to think about the fact that what he had chosen to do that day had led to him violating one of his parents' firmest rules.

He never really thought about it until his four-legged companion left him. The dog, which did not belong to the little boy, had found something else to occupy his time and had gone off in another pursuit.

For the first time since this entire experience began, the little boy was very aware of his surroundings. They were totally unfamiliar to him. He was also aware of the fact that he had disobeyed his parents, but that wasn't really his major concern at the moment.

As he stood there caught up in thorns and briers in an unfamiliar wooded area, he was very aware of one very frightening thing. His stomach churned as he realized that he was lost!

He did not know where he was. He was not sure how he got there. He certainly did not know the way back to the safety of his home. There was nobody to talk to, to offer advice, or to guide him out of wherever it was that he found himself. He was just across the road from his house, but he might as well have been a million miles away.

He was lost!

One of the best sounds this little boy ever heard was the voice of his father calling his name. His father and some other men had started looking for him as soon as it was discovered that he was lost. In fact, as he learned later, since the family lived fairly close to a small airport, somebody had volunteered to look for him from the air.

He learned something else later, too. He learned that there was an old abandoned well in that woods. It was covered by leaves and fallen branches and was almost impossible to see. The little boy's father and mother told him that his tracks had come extremely close to that old well. He had never even seen that well.

What kind of punishment did our little adventurer receive for violating his parents' strict warnings? As he looks back over more than six decades, he can't remember. What he does remember is how he felt as he heard the voice of his father and how good it was to be safe in his home and to be no longer lost.

On three different occasions, Jesus spoke of the reason for His coming as a rescue mission. Some manuscripts do not have the reference given at the beginning of this chapter from Matthew 18:11. For that reason, some translations also do not include it in Matthew's account and/or include it as a marginal reading. If the omission of Matthew 18:11 is correct, then this is not the next statement Jesus made about the reason for His coming. For the purpose of this book, however, we will discuss it next and will consider the other two passages cited at the beginning of this chapter as well.

It is intriguing to notice how each of the verses begins in which Jesus gave the reason for His coming as being connected to saving the lost. In each instance, the verse begins with the word "for."

There must be some connection to His statement(s) and the surrounding events and circumstances. Hopefully, our understanding of what Jesus said and how we can apply His statements to our lives can be enhanced as we consider, even briefly, the circumstances surrounding each one.

It is interesting to notice that the statement in Matthew 18:11 is sandwiched between some interesting material. Matthew 18 begins with our Lord's disciples asking the following question: "Who then is greatest in the kingdom of heaven?" (v. 1). This question prompted Jesus to discuss the importance of humility. He also warned against offending or causing to stumble "one of these little ones who believe in Me" (v. 6). There is also a discussion about the type of purity and sacrifice He expects from His followers.

In the material following verse 11, we find something similar to what we can find in Luke 15. There are some differences, but, in both passages, one lost soul is compared to a lost sheep belonging to a man who had a hundred sheep. It is in this context, too, that we find our Lord's instruction about what to do "if your brother sins against you" (Matt. 18:15). We may remember that this "process" ends with the man being considered "like a heathen and a tax collector" (Matt. 18:17) if he refuses to repent.

The account recorded in Luke 9 involves a village of the Samaritans who did not receive Jesus, even though He had sent messengers ahead of Him to prepare for His coming. The reaction of the brothers who were known as "the sons of thunder" can be seen in the question they asked at that time: "Lord, do You want us to command fire to come down from heaven and consume them, just as Elijah did?" (Luke 9:54).

The events of Luke 19 are probably the most familiar of all of these incidents. Small children learn the song about the "wee little man" named Zacchaeus. After, in a sense, inviting Himself to the house of Zacchaeus, Jesus had a conversation with him. Following that conversation, Jesus said, "Today salvation has come to this house, because he also is a son of Abraham; for the Son of Man has come to seek and to save that which was lost" (Luke 19:9-10).

If these three different accounts of three different circumstances teach us anything, they teach us at least one very important thing. People from all walks of life and in various circumstances in life need a Savior and, without Jesus as their Savior, they are lost!

Probably no thought about why Jesus came should affect us as deeply as this one. We need to come face to face with the sobering thought that without Jesus we are lost. We normally do not like to think of ourselves in that way. In fact, all too often, we do not take the time to think of our spiritual condition at all. We may, like the disciples of Matthew 18, be jockeying for, or at least wondering about, greatness in the kingdom. In so doing, we may overlook or mistreat some "little ones" and let our guards down when it comes to personal devotion and purity. We may even become so calloused that the fact that we are no longer in fellowship with God's people or God, Himself, means very little to us.

Our attitudes can become similar to the attitudes exhibited by James and John in Luke 9. We may see those who are unreceptive as good for nothing except to be destroyed. It is sad to lose sight of the truth that they are precious souls who need to be taught.

The third chapter of John contains some material that may be the best commentary on Luke 9 that can be found anywhere. The favorite verse of millions of people is John 3:16 which speaks of God's great love that prompted the greatest gift to accomplish the greatest rescue mission ever known. All too often, we may overlook the following verse, which informs us, "For God did not send His Son into the world to condemn the world, but that the world through Him might be saved" (John 3:17). The reason why Jesus did not come to condemn the people in the world is explained in verse 18. They were (and are) "condemned already" without Jesus.

The last set of circumstances, found in Luke 19, involves a man (Zacchaeus) who, as the chapter opens, does not appear to be a follower of Jesus. He was curious about Him and took some pains to see Him, but was not yet a disciple.

Interestingly, it is in this context that the words of Jesus turn His mission from a rescue mission to a search and rescue mission. This is the first time we find our Lord saying, "for the Son of Man has come to seek and to save that which was lost" (Luke 19:10). This has serious implications for the Lord's body. If we are to be about carrying out His will, we will be actively seeking all those who are outside the fold of safety.

Gone will be the days when we see our responsibility as being met when we plan a gospel meeting, secure a speaker, advertise it, and wait for people to show up. Gone will be the days when we sit in our padded pews on Sunday and our recliners Monday through Saturday. Paul caught the spirit of what is important. That is why he was able to remind the Ephesian elders that he "taught... publicly and from house to house" (Acts 20:20).

I can still vividly recall seeing a church bus driving around my hometown years ago. The color was not eye-catching. It was sort of a drab, nondescript blue. It was the white lettering that caught my attention. The letters identified the group and the address where they worshiped (just two doors down from the house in which my wife grew up) and then declared that church to be "The Church with Acts 20:20 Vision."

One of the reasons I remember that so vividly is that the bus belonged to a church that was part of the religious organization I left when I became a member of the Lord's church. Here was a group wearing a name they cannot find in the Bible, teaching a "plan of salvation" not found in the Bible, and organized in a way not found in God's Word and yet, at the same time, claiming to follow Paul's example in Acts 20:20!

The church of Christ needs to be the church with Acts 20:20 vision. We need to be on the same "search and rescue mission" our Lord was on.

You may want to put this book down at this point and pull out a sheet of paper and a pencil. I'm asking each of us to make a list of what we consider to be the greatest problems facing the Lord's church in our day and time. What would your list include? Would some or all of the following be there?

- Liberalism
- Legalism
- Materialism
- Worldliness
- Apathy
- Indifference
- False teachers and teachings
- Lack of sacrificial giving
- Lack of sacrificial living
- Sin in the camp

Is your list longer than that? I'm sure that, if space would allow, we could fill up many, many pages with problems, concerns, and challenges faced by the church today.

I would like to make a "nomination" for that list that has not yet appeared in this discussion. Could it be that the following things could explain why many of us do not see the need to reach and teach others?

- I don't fully understand what it means to be lost.
- I really do not think that those outside of Christ actually are lost.
- I have never considered the fact that I could be lost if I do not do my part in helping to "seek and to save that which was lost."

Isn't it interesting that, in each case where Jesus speaks of Himself as coming to save the lost, He speaks of Himself as "the Son of Man"? Read carefully Hebrews 2:14-18. In this passage, as well as many others, the humanity of Jesus is stressed. Also in this passage, as well as others, one of the reasons for His humanity is discussed. Jesus needed to be one of us. He could not fulfill His mission in any other way. All of this makes for interesting religious discussion about the nature of our Lord. It also should point us to interesting discussions about our role as His body.

If we are to seek and save the lost, we need to be with the lost. No, we cannot "continue in sin that grace may abound" (Rom. 6:1), but neither can we reach those who do not have a proper relationship with our Lord if we never have any contact with them.

It is easy to overlook what I believe to be very important details about two of the passages we have been looking at in this chapter. These details may change our perspective somewhat and, hopefully, challenge us a great deal.

First, in the account found in Matthew 18, the man who "refuses even to hear the church [is to be considered as] a heathen and a tax collector." (v. 17). Does this mean that there is to be absolutely no contact? That is how the Pharisees treated those whom they considered to be heathens and publicans.

However, Jesus treated these people differently and, as is very apparent in the Gospels, was severely criticized for so doing. Our Lord associated with these people for the purpose of offering them the only hope they had. He did not, as did James and John, see them as only fit for destruction. He saw lost sheep who needed a Shepherd.

It seems that those who are "outside of our fellowship" need to be taught. They may have never been a Christian or they may be back in the world after once having served the Lord. Whichever of these is the case, they need somebody to care enough to teach and persuade them.

The incident in which James and John were involved also has an easily overlooked, but very important, component. The last sentence of Luke 9:56 is rich with implications. The record says, "And they went to another village."

It may very well be that Jesus knew that the first village would never be receptive. While there was no need to destroy it, there was a real need to keep reaching and teaching. The people in the next village might well have been more receptive than those in the first village. Our Lord did not, nor can we afford to, allow one failure, or even a succession of failures, keep us from doing what He has commanded that we do. To use the analogy used by Paul, our task is to plant and water and to depend upon God for the increase (cf. 1 Cor. 3:7).

That little boy who followed that dog over six decades ago will never forget the panic he felt when he realized he was absolutely and totally lost. The word "despair" does not come close to describing his state of mind on that day. Neither do words like "relief," "gratitude," or "joy" adequately describe how he felt when he heard his father's voice and was returned to the safety of his home. He was back where he needed to be and wanted to be. He knew that somebody loved him enough to search for him and to save him from dangers about which he was totally unaware. He was even more than willing to accept whatever punishment his parents thought might be appropriate. Apparently, though, the parents thought that he had suffered enough and had learned a valuable lesson. After experiencing the pain, fear, and isolation of being lost, he now rejoiced in the comfort, love, and security of being home. He "once was lost, but now was found."

All of this was true because of parents who loved him deeply and were not content to merely let him find his way back home. They were willing to seek until they found their son. It was also true because people who knew of the love those parents had for their son were willing to give of their time and energy to bring that boy back to safety. There were other things they could have been doing that day, but none more important than returning a small boy back to his home.

That boy had no way of knowing that, a few years later, he would begin dating a Christian young lady who, with the help of others, patiently and lovingly helped to rescue him in a far more significant way. During the years when they dated, and even during the first few years of their marriage, she was aware of something about which he was unaware—or at least was unwilling to admit.

Although he thought things were going pretty well in his life and in their life together, she recognized the fact that he was lost in a way far more serious and dangerous than had been the case when he was a little boy. He had not meant to be lost. In fact, he did not really think he was lost for quite a while, but, because of her influence and the influence of some others, he began to take stock of where he was spiritually.

That little boy who followed a dog into some woods had no idea that, years later, he would feel that same sense of despondency and urgency that he felt in those woods. This time, it was a much more serious sense of despondency. This time, it was a different Father whose voice he heard as the gospel had an impact on his life.

In some ways, that person who was now a young man was like the apostle Paul in that he had been reared in a very religious setting and was satisfied where he was. Like Paul, he came to the realization that "Christ Jesus came into the world to save sinners, of whom I am chief" (1 Tim. 1:15). The gospel invitation was for him, after all. It was not just for somebody else. He was lost, and he needed a Savior.

One night, he did something he thought he would never do. He had been immersed as a teenager, but he now understood that the teaching he had obeyed did not correspond to the teaching of the New Testament. He was no longer satisfied with that and on this night decided to be baptized into Christ for the remission of his sins (cf. Acts 2:38, Gal. 3:27, Rom. 6:3ff., 1 Pet. 3:21).

That was not the last time he did something he thought he would never do. Who would have ever thought that a little boy who followed a dog into the woods would someday leave a profession he had chosen, move from his hometown, and spend the rest of his life trying to preach and teach others? Who would have thought that he would someday be writing these words?

I am very grateful that somebody cared enough about me when I was lost in the woods. I am eternally grateful that somebody thought enough about me to teach me when my soul was lost.

I keep asking myself if I care enough about others. I sometimes wonder if I'm doing my part to "seek and save the lost."

How about you? Is your salvation a personal matter or were you, as one man told me one time, "inducted into the family religion"? Is there a real sense that you were saved, or that you just became a part of something by meeting its membership requirements?

Have you really found your way home? Do you care enough to help others find their way? We have no idea what can happen if we take seriously and personally the challenge to seek and save the lost.

8

"FOR JUDGMENT I HAVE COME INTO THIS WORLD"

JOHN 9:39

Most, if not all, of us have seen the picture above at one time or another. What we see in the picture depends on our perspective. Some of us will first see an attractive young lady looking off into the distance. The one who is viewing the picture and seeing that image is, in effect, standing behind her and looking over her left shoulder. The bonnet on her head is a complement to her long, flowing hair that is brushed back attractively in a manner that barely allows part of her left ear to be seen.

The cute little upturned nose captures our attention.

Wait! Is that a cute upturned nose or is it a wart on a large unattractive nose of an equally unattractive woman? Is that an ear of an attractive young lady or an eye of a woman who almost looks witchlike? That line that looked like a necklace around the neck of the young lady could be the mouth of the older lady, couldn't it? The long, flowing hair loses much of its appeal also; especially when some of it now resembles wrinkles and sagging skin more than hair.

What do you see when you look at Jesus? What do you like to consider when you think about His mission? Many of us would rather consider the One who said that His mission was all about some of the statements we've already taken a look at in this book. We would rather not think much about the fact that Jesus said, "For judgment I am come into this world" (John 9:39).

In a way that is similar to taking a second look at the picture, we would be well advised to take a second look at our Lord's mission. We need to remember that Paul told all who read the letter to the Romans to "consider the goodness and severity of God" (Rom. 11:22).

We probably remember the background and context of the statement of Jesus found in John 9:39. The account of the healing of the man who was born blind is well known. Some interesting questions are touched on in this chapter. For example, the relationship between suffering and sin is explored here. Even Jesus' own disciples thought that the man's blindness must have been the result of somebody's sin (cf. v. 2). Echoes of Job's "friends" are heard here. They are also heard every time one of us asks, "What did I do to deserve this?"

John 9:31 is also a source of more than a little discussion. When the subject of prayer comes up in any discussion and, when that discussion turns to who has the right to expect prayers to be heard and answered, we can be sure that somebody will refer to the statement made by the (formerly) blind man, "Now we know that God does not hear sinners; but if anyone is a worshiper of God and does His will, He hears him."

Somebody in that discussion will remind those involved that, though John's record of the statement is inspired, the man making the statement is not inspired. Somebody else will bring the case of Cornelius into the discussion, and people will be asked to make a judgment about the difference between a prayer being heard and prayers "...com(ing) up for a memorial before God" (Acts 10:4). The discussion goes on and on from this point.

It may seem to be a simplistic approach to this discussion, but it seems that a better use of our time would be to make sure that my relationship with God is such that, when I address Him as "Father," there is no doubt about that fact. If we would spend our time like that and would do what we could to encourage others to have that relationship, we might not have quite as much time to involve ourselves in a lot of discussions which are, in many cases, just a "rehash" of positions people have held for years and years.

Of course, as was so often the case when Jesus performed a miracle and/or taught the people, His Jewish detractors were right there to scrutinize and criticize. The events recorded in John 9 are certainly no exception to this.

The Jews used a variety of tactics this time. They were critical of this action being taken on a Sabbath day; they questioned whether or not this was the same man who was born blind; they interrogated the man and his parents; and they finally did what the parents had feared would happen to them; they "cast him out" (v. 35). It was at this point that Jesus had a short conversation with the man who had been healed. The conversation had this result: "And he [the man who had been healed] said, 'Lord, I believe!' And he worshiped Him" (v. 38).

Then Jesus made the statement about coming into the world for judgment. The entire verse written by John states: "And Jesus said, 'For judgment I have come into this world, that those who do not see may see, and that those who see may be made blind'" (John 9:39).

"Judgment" is a word we seemingly do not hear much about in our day and time. We like to look at the "pretty young lady" in the picture. We don't like to focus on the "ugly old woman." We may try to soften the effect of these words from the lips of our Lord by hoping that this word, as used in this instance, may not have a negative connotation. After all, not every judgment is a negative judgment. Sometimes in the judgment of some court or judge, a person may be granted his or her freedom or awarded a large sum of money.

However, the Greek word that is used here does not give us much hope that this would be the case. It is rendered by two other English words in the New Testament. When it is not translated "judgment," it is translated as either "condemnation" or "damnation."

It is interesting and sobering to consider the fact that one of those places is in James 3:1, where James warns, "My brethren, be not many masters, knowing that we shall receive the greater condemnation" (KJV). The NKJV has the word "teachers" for "masters" and the word "judgment" for "condemnation." It doesn't matter a great deal which words we use in this instance. The meaning is very clear. Those who preach and teach God's Word need to do so with the awareness that they will answer for what they teach and/or preach.

It needs to be remembered that Paul was well aware of the fact that every facet of his life would be examined, even though he was an inspired man. It may be argued that the major thrust of his words in 1 Cor. 9:27 was not necessarily what he taught, but, it seems to me that they would be included in his statement that "I discipline my body and bring it into subjection, lest, when I have preached to others, I myself should become disqualified."

Is Paul writing only about those who heard his preaching, or is he including himself in 2 Corinthians 5:11, when he wrote, "Knowing therefore, the terror of the Lord, we persuade men"? Since, in the verse just prior to that one, he did not write that "you must all appear before the judgment seat of Christ," but that "we must all appear before the judgment seat of Christ, that each one may receive the things done in the body, according to what he has done, whether good or bad" (2 Cor. 5:10), it would appear that he understood the weighty responsibility that was his as he taught.

At the same time, those who hear preaching and teaching from God's Word need to be impressed with the fact that there will, in fact, be a judgment. Lessons are vitally needed on numerous subjects that will help us in our relationships with one another and with God in this life. It is true that the Bible is, and always will be, the best "manual" for problem-solving, marital relationships, relationships between and among Christians, proper attitudes, morality, etc. The list could go on and on. It is also true that the best material for such subjects as prayer, church growth, personal commitment, etc. is found in God's Word. All of the books that have been written on any of these subjects serve only to comment on what God has already revealed.

However, we do ourselves and others a terrible disservice if we do not impress upon them the truth that "godliness is profitable for all things, having promise of the life that now is and of that which is to come" (1 Tim. 4:8).

We will not take the time or space here to try to refer to each passage that speaks of a future judgment. Many of them come to mind easily to those who have a working knowledge of the Bible. Suffice it to say that the Bible teaches clearly and forcefully that to which we have already referred in 2 Corinthians 5:10. Indeed, each one of us will stand before our Lord in judgment. For some, it will be a day of great joy. For others, the horror of that day and its consequences are beyond our imagination.

However, in John 9, Jesus indicated that His coming into the world the first time was a time of judgment. In this passage, He did not say that He was coming back to judge the world, though that is, as we have already suggested, unmistakably true. Consider His words again: "For judgment I have come into this world" (John 9:39). A question may come to mind at this point. Did He not also say in John 3 that "God did not send His Son into the world to condemn the world, but that the world through

Him might be saved" (John 3:17)? How can both of these statements be true? How can it be true that our Lord was sent to save the world and to condemn the world at the same time?

The answer to those questions may lie in His statements about who could see and who could not see in John 9:39. You will remember that Jesus was once called upon to take part in a synagogue service in his hometown of Nazareth on one occasion. When He was given the book of Isaiah, He read from Isaiah 61:1-2 and declared that, "Today this Scripture is fulfilled in your hearing" (Luke 4:21).

There is an interesting and somewhat puzzling element to all of this. One of the things that Luke records that Jesus read was "recovering of sight to the blind" (Luke 4:18). When one looks at the passage as it is found in Isaiah 61, though, that statement is not to be found. It may be of more than casual interest and importance to notice where Jesus placed that statement. It is found between these two statements which are, without question, found in Isaiah 61:1—

"To proclaim liberty to the captives"

"And the opening of the prison to those who are bound"

When I was younger, a popular expression (which we thought was somehow very cool) was, "'I see,' said the blind man." When somebody explained something to you and you finally "got it," you were likely to use that expression. I never, in my wildest imagination, thought that this expression would help someday to explain a passage of scripture, but I believe it does! Two things happened in John 9 concerning a man who was physically blind.

First, he was no longer hindered by that terrible malady. He could see God's creation for the first time! (Remember he had been born blind.) He could see the faces of those who, up to that point, he only knew by the sound of their voices and/or possibly their touch.

Secondly, and more significantly, this man who had been born blind was no longer blinded spiritually by the prejudices of those Jewish "authorities" who were critical of him and of the One who had healed him. He, and all of the Jews of his day, had been captive to their interpretation of the law and were oppressed by these men who claimed to be "Moses' disciples" (John 9:28). Now, because he had listened to Jesus' claims and had decided for himself, he really could "see." This was truly a great day for him on so many levels!

However, what about the critics? What about those who claimed to have all of the answers? It seems there is some significance in the fact that Jesus said that "those who see may be made blind" (John 9:39). Was He saying that His coming to earth would make their condition worse?

I believe that this is exactly what He was saying! Further, I believe that this understanding of the statement is in keeping with some prophecies. You will remember that Isaiah's mission was not an altogether pleasant one. After he had volunteered to be God's spokesman (Isa. 6:8), he was told that his preaching would make people less receptive, not more receptive. Consider carefully the language of Isaiah 6:9-10: "And He said, 'Go, and tell this people: 'Keep on hearing, but do not understand; Keep on seeing, but do not perceive.' Make the heart of this people dull, And their ears heavy, And shut their eyes; Lest they see with their eyes, And hear with their ears, And understand with their heart, And return and be healed."

Although God told Isaiah that this was true of his contemporaries, Jesus also told the people of His day that these words applied to them. In Matthew 13, when His disciples asked why He taught in parables, He told them about two classes of people.

First, there were people living during that time just like the people of Isaiah's time. They were closing their eyes and, in so doing, their hearts kept getting more hardened (v. 15). The effect of this was that the more Jesus taught, the more they rejected Him. They were being "made blind" by their own prejudices, self-righteousness, and arrogance.

However, there were others who were described by Jesus in this manner: "But blessed are your eyes for they see, and your ears for they hear" (Matt. 13:16). They, like the man born blind, listened to what Jesus had to say with "honest and good heart" (Luke 8:15). They were not swayed by the threats of those who set themselves up as religious authorities. They made up their own minds!

This discussion is very reminiscent of a similar one that involves an Old Testament character. Occasionally the question will be raised about the hardening of Pharaoh's heart. There are passages in the book of Exodus that informs us that God says that He will do the hardening. One such example is Exodus 4:21—"And the LORD said to Moses, 'When you go back to Egypt, see that you do all those wonders before Pharaoh which I have put in your hand. But I will harden his heart, so that he will not let the people go.'"

However, in Exodus 8:15 it is written that "when Pharaoh saw that there was relief, he hardened his heart and did not heed them, as the LORD had said." So, what's the answer to the question? Who hardened Pharaoh's heart? Was it God or was it Pharaoh? The answer is, "Yes!" Both God and Pharaoh hardened Pharaoh's heart. God continually gave to Pharaoh more than adequate proof of His identity and power. He kept giving Pharaoh repeated opportunities to "do the right thing." In fact, there were times when Pharaoh would actually do what was right only to change his mind later.

Every time Pharaoh decided to further oppress God's people and/or made some other unwise choice, his heart got just that much harder. Every time he made such a decision, it made it easier to make a similar decision in the future.

As suggested earlier, this series of events involving God and Pharaoh may help to explain how Jesus could speak of some who lived during His time on earth. As Isaiah had prophesied, preaching would help to harden their hearts and close their eyes.

As we reconsider the connection between John 9 and John 3, we remember that Jesus' statement did not end with Him saying that His

Father "did not send His Son into the world to condemn the world, but that the world through Him might be saved." Even in this passage, there is a clear and forceful reference to condemnation which was associated with His coming into the world the first time. He was not looking into the far distant future, but was speaking of people who were His contemporaries when He said:

> He who believes in Him is not condemned; but he who does not believe is condemned already, because he has not believed in the name of the only begotten Son of God. And this is the condemnation, that the light has come into the world, and men loved darkness rather than light, because their deeds were evil. For everyone practicing evil hates the light and does not come to the light, lest his deeds should be exposed. But he who does the truth comes to the light, that his deeds may be clearly seen, that they have been done in God.
>
> John 3:18-21

As has already been suggested, when Jesus walked among men, there were two classes of people. The difference had nothing to do with race, nationality, economic or educational levels, or any of the other "barriers" we sometimes put between us. The difference was seen in how receptive they were to His teachings. Some "hate[d] the light and [did] not come to the light" (John 3:20). Others "[did] the truth [and came] to the light" (John 3:20).

The situation had not changed when Paul wrote these words in 2 Corinthians 2:15-16—"For we are to God the fragrance of Christ among those who are being saved and among those who are perishing. To the one we are the aroma of death leading to death, and to the other the aroma of life leading to life. And who is sufficient for these things?"

If people could "close their eyes" to God's message in the days of Isaiah, the days during our Lord's earthly ministry, and during Paul's ministry, could the same thing be happening today? Could people today become increasingly blind to their spiritual condition and their need for a Savior? Sadly, the answer is, "Yes."

The inspired words of Paul found in 2 Corinthians 4:3-4 sound like a description of the society in which we find ourselves as much as the society in which Paul lived: "But even if our gospel is veiled, it is veiled to those who are perishing, whose minds the god of this age has blinded, who do not believe, lest the light of the gospel of the glory of Christ, who is the image of God, should shine on them."

Are there not millions in our time who have been "blinded" by the sparkle of diamonds and gold, the bright lights of Hollywood or Las Vegas (or a nearby location with similar allure), the surface beauty of somebody who would entice us to abandon our morals, and/or a variety of other pursuits and interests? Do we not all know people who are "too busy" making a living, making sure they and their children are involved in every social and recreational activity available, and/or having a good time to seriously consider their relationship with God and their responsibility to Him? Do I see one of those people when I look into the mirror?

Sadly, many who have been baptized into Christ (cf. Rom. 6:3, Gal. 3:27) could later become spiritually blind. While some in religious circles minimize the importance of baptism, I am afraid that others may ascribe to this act of obedience qualities which it does not have. Baptism is not some sort of eye salve that makes us forever immune to the allure of the world and/or other factors which might take our focus off of the Lord.

The "Christian Graces" about which Peter writes in 2 Peter 1:5-7 are fairly well known by all who read the Bible. Likewise, the positive results of making sure that they are a once a part of our lives are familiar, encouraging, and challenging: "For if these things are yours and abound, you will be neither barren nor unfruitful in the knowledge of our Lord Jesus Christ" (2 Pet. 1:8).

However, what happens if these things are not ours? What if they do not abound? The Holy Spirit's language is clear. The language also fits the discussion about spiritual blindness. We need to read carefully these words: "For he who lacks these things is shortsighted, even to blindness, and has forgotten that he was cleansed from his old sins" (2 Pet. 1:9).

The lesson is clear; our vision must be clear and our focus must be singular. In the words of the writer of Hebrews, "Wherefore seeing we also are compassed about with so great a cloud of witnesses, let us lay aside every weight, and the sin which doth so easily beset us, and let us run with patience the race that is set before us, Looking unto Jesus the author and finisher of our faith; who for the joy that was set before him endured the cross, despising the shame, and is set down at the right hand of the throne of God" (Heb. 12:1-2).

If that is our focus and our goal, the concept of judgment should not frighten us—now or in the future!

9

""I HAVE COME THAT THEY MIGHT HAVE LIFE, AND THAT THEY MIGHT HAVE IT MORE ABUNDANTLY"

JOHN 10:10

In a very real sense, this chapter is a continuation of the previous chapter. The chapter break between John 9:41 and 10:1 is unfortunate. This material is still part of that confrontation that Jesus was having with His critics concerning the healing of the man who had been born blind.

When viewed from this perspective, there is quite a contrast to be seen. On one hand, there are the Pharisees who blinded themselves to the teachings of Jesus. On the other hand, there are the people and the relationship described in John 10. The extremely close relationship that a shepherd of that day had with his sheep was the model for the relationship that Jesus used to describe His relationship with His followers.

The tenth chapter of John lends itself to a variety of avenues of study, all of which have some degree of merit. Some of the studies are of a practical nature, others of more of a doctrinal nature, and some contain elements of both. What we propose to do here is to try to find some clues to the meaning of an abundant life.

I'm afraid that the following scenario could describe many as they (we) look for an abundant life:

I sat down and looked through some magazines this past week. I discovered that if I want to feel right, I need to get a NordicTrack. I don't have a NordicTrack, just a membership down at the gym, so I suddenly realized that I didn't feel as healthy as I thought I did.

I then read that if I wanted to be stylish, I would need to buy a Toyota Camry. Our family van was in the shop, so I had been driving our old Mercury Sable. That felt bad enough. Real men drive SUVs or bright red sports cars. I've got four kids, so I don't have the luxury of driving what real men drive. So I found out that I couldn't be stylish with the cars I owned.

Then I saw that if I wanted to really feel the spring season, I had to dress for the spring season, and the only place for that was at Dillard's. I knew I wouldn't have a chance to go to Dillard's that week. Suddenly the beautiful weather just didn't seem that beautiful. I just wasn't dressed for it.

It didn't get any better. I learned that I needed to be opening my mail with a knife from Oneida. I only had a two-dollar letter opener from Office Depot. Now even my mail was disappointing. On top of that, I discovered that I couldn't have a good meal if I wasn't in Texas – at least not a meal that would satisfy me. So much for my Lean Cuisines. Then I read that if I wanted to be a man, at least a manlier man than my neighbor, I had to drive a Yard-Man mower with a Briggs and Stratton engine. At least it was cheaper than a new SUV.

I liked my house until I saw the new development's ad. I thought my family and I were close until I realized we didn't have season passes to the amusement park. I even thought I loved my wife, but since I hadn't bought her a diamond necklace from the jewelry store, I was informed that I didn't. I found out that I can't even be romantic with my wife unless we use Sylvania light bulbs. Wouldn't you know, we have GE.

By the time I got finished with those magazines, I wasn't

> just depressed – I needed counseling. Ever felt that way? We all have. It's the sad fruit of living a life that covets.[1]

As I type these words, I am thinking of two men who are very dear friends of mine. Both are faithful and dedicated gospel preachers. Each is dealing with situations that are very heavy burdens for them. Some of those burdens are related to family matters; some are related to the churches where they labor; some are personal. Is it possible that they could be living an abundant life?

Each one of us has situations in our lives that are far less than "optimal." Can we still have an abundant life as we deal with them? It is my conviction that the answer given in John 10 is an emphatic "yes."

Many who have heard me preach would tell you that John 10 is my "go-to passage" as I attempt to evaluate myself as an elder (shepherd) in the Lord's church. I am constantly seeking to emulate the Good Shepherd and His love and concern for His sheep. However, that is not the focus of this chapter in this book. The material I am presenting here should be my "go-to passage" as a Christian (one of the Lord's sheep). It is my prayer that what I write here will encourage all of us and, at the same time, challenge each of us to live an abundant life.

If, as the illustration indicates, "one's life does not consist in the abundance of his possessions" (Luke 12:15), where is the abundant life to be found? I believe it is to be found in the relationship described in the chapter under consideration. As I read the words of John 10, I get the distinct impression that those who live the abundant life...

FOLLOW THE GOOD SHEPHERD (vv. 4, 27)

In human terms, the thieves and robbers (cf. v. 8) are "in it for the money." They are not to be followed. It is truly sad that so many are

1. http://www.sermoncentral.com/illustrations/sermon-illustration-humor-lifesseasons-covet-contentment-8362.asp

following some who seem to be no more than religious hucksters and charlatans. With very little research, one can find a fairly long list of religious leaders who live "the lifestyle of the rich and famous," and who are, at the same time, constantly and consistently begging for monetary donations.

We must also point out that the best of human shepherds are just that; human shepherds. Even those with the very best of intentions will make mistakes. Humans can and will disappoint. Even unintentionally, humans can lead others in the wrong direction. The only shepherd that truly can provide an abundant life is the one who was willing to "lay down [His] life for the sheep" (v. 11). That, in itself, should provide us with adequate motivation to follow Him.

KNOW THE GOOD SHEPHERD (vv. 14, 27)

It is entirely possible to follow somebody one does not know. You may have a favorite author, performer, politician, etc. In a sense, it could be said that you "follow" that person. Does that mean you know him/her?

Are there not people in your life whom you don't really know? In my case, I know people in my neighborhood and in other neighborhoods and communities in which I have lived. I do not know them like I know the people who have lived under the same roof as I have; with whom I have spent a great deal of quality time; whom I've made an effort to get to know.

Consider these words from the inspired pen of Paul: "that I may know Him" (Phil. 3:10). A man of great worldly and religious ambition earlier in life now had a goal of knowing the Good Shepherd. Both the wording of that verse and the entirety of Paul's life are testimonies to the fact that the kind of knowledge being discussed here is not fixed and/or static. It is an ongoing and growing process.

This kind of knowledge is also not about knowing only facts. It is about knowing a person. All of us know a lot of facts about a lot of people we've never even met, much less claim to know.

It is sobering to consider that knowing or believing the facts is not to be equated with living the kind of life Jesus is describing in John 10. His own half-brothers knew facts about Him and even in some sense knew Him. John 7:5 reminds us that, at least at this point in their lives, "not even His brothers believed in Him." The religious leaders described in John 12:42-43 "believed in Him" It cannot be successfully argued, however, that they were part of His fold since "...they loved the glory that comes from man more than the glory that comes from God."

How do I know that I know the Good Shepherd? It seems that a very strong indicator is that those who live an abundant life...

KNOW THE VOICE OF THE GOOD SHEPHERD (vv. 3-4, 27)

It has been over a decade since my parents departed this life, yet I can still "hear" their voices. I had that kind of relationship with them. I am certain that there are people in all of our lives whose voices we know instantly when we hear them. We've been with them a lot. We've shared our lives together. We know each other intimately in the best meaning of that word. Time and effort has been spent in "relationship building."

John 6 is an interesting study in many ways. Jesus had attracted a large following, due in no small part to His feeding of the five thousand. It could be said that these people followed Him; that they knew Him; that they knew His voice. However, not all of them knew His voice in the same way. What they heard that voice say provoked two totally different reactions.

The first is found in verse 66: "After this many of His disciples turned back and no longer walked with Him." These were those who knew that the voice of Jesus was the voice of the One who could (and had) met a temporary physical need (cf. John 6:26).

The second reaction is stated by Peter. I think most of us would agree that, at least in some respects, we can identify with Peter. If in no other way, we can identify with some of his flaws. Hopefully, too, we can identify with his desire to be a true and loyal follower of the Good Shepherd. It was this flawed follower who said to Jesus, "You have the words of eternal life, and we have believed, and have come to know that you are the Holy One of God" (v. 69).

Peter did not, like many of the religious leaders, listen to Jesus only to criticize. He did not, as was the case with some who heard Paul later, listen only "to hear some new thing" (Acts 17:21). Peter appears to be one who was listening to the voice of One whom he loved supremely. He was listening to One to whom he had dedicated His life. He was listening to learn, to obey, and to model. In every good sense of the word, he knew the voice of Jesus.

In case somebody would object that we cannot actually hear the voice of Jesus today, I would submit that many who actually did hear his voice never came to know his voice in the sense that we are discussing here. I would also suggest that a reading of John 20:30-31 might be appropriate. If John wrote his gospel for us to have "life in His name," would we not be wise to spend time allowing the Lord to communicate with us through His word?

Maybe I need to ask myself how much time I spend reading, studying, assimilating, and applying the Word. My answer might give me an indication of how abundant my life truly is.

MAKE A DECISION/COMMITMENT

Why did my father make sure his hair was combed and "everything was in place" when he was going to be around my mother who no longer really knew who she was, much less who he was? Why have my two preacher friends I mentioned earlier never given any thought to not serving the Lord any longer (in at least some capacity).

Why do I see people who can barely get around at almost every one of the assemblies where I preach? Why do I hear about those same people "doing what they can" for the Lord during the week? Is it not because they have, in the words of a song, "decided to follow Jesus"? Why do I hear about and/or see evidence of church members who have time, energy, and money for pursuing things of no spiritual value at all? Why do all of us know of some who were, at one time, faithful to the Lord, but who can no longer be described that way?

The answer to all of those questions lies in the firmness of a decision and the resolve involved in a commitment. I'm sure that many of His day considered Jesus to be some sort of "itinerant preacher." Most of us would consider the world and the environment in which He lived while on earth to be fairly primitive by our modern standards. He appeared to have little, if anything, to offer as far as material interests were concerned. After all, He said himself that "the Son of Man has nowhere to lay His head" (Matt. 8:20).

Those facts help to bolster the idea that an abundant life is not the result of circumstances. Along with that, He was described prophetically in this manner: "He is despised and rejected by men. A Man of sorrows and acquainted with grief" (Isa. 53:3).

The abundant life is about relationship. Specifically, it is about a relationship with Jesus.

It seems to me that, long ago, this relationship was beautifully described in Psalm 23. As I read that description, I will learn that, if the Lord is, indeed, my shepherd, I will...

TALK TO OTHERS

I will tell them, "The Lord is my shepherd; I shall not want. He makes me to lie down in green pastures. He leads me beside the still waters. He restores my soul. He leads me in the paths of righteousness for His name's sake."

TALK TO HIM

I will say to Him, "Even though I walk through the valley of the shadow of death, I will fear no evil, for you are with me; your rod and your staff, they comfort me. You prepare a table before me in the presence of my enemies; you anoint my head with oil; my cup overflows."

TALK TO MYSELF

I will remind myself, "Surely goodness and mercy shall follow me all the days of my life, and I shall dwell in the house of the Lord forever."

All of that sure sounds like an abundant life to me! The bottom line is that only I can decide if I want to live an abundant life on the world's terms or on terms laid down by the Good Shepherd. As much as family members, elders, preachers, and others would like to make the decision/commitment for me, it has to be my decision.

Am I—are you—included in the following description? Do I—you—have the assurance found here? "My sheep hear my voice, and I know them, and they follow Me. And I give them eternal life, and they shall never perish; neither shall anyone snatch them out of my hand" (John 10:27-28).

10

"JUST AS THE SON OF MAN DID NOT COME TO BE SERVED, BUT TO SERVE, AND TO GIVE HIS LIFE A RANSOM FOR MANY"

MATTHEW 20:28

It was becoming more and more apparent to at least some of the followers of our Lord that the time was approaching when some of His predictions were about to come true. We can be sure that they did not want to hear about His suffering and death, nor did they look forward to the actual events themselves.

However, both His teachings and the events they were witnessing surely were enough to convince them that the time was, in fact, drawing near. No doubt, they had many questions for which they still would like to have answers.

Many who read these words and the one who is writing them have been in the position of watching a loved one's health deteriorate. One of the things many do in these situations is to try to have those "heart to heart talks." Even when that is done, we often wish we could still discuss some things with that loved one after he or she has passed on into eternity.

Apparently, one of the things on the mind of some of Jesus' followers was His predictions about His kingdom. They were aware of some Old Testament prophecies that indicated that the coming Messiah would usher in His reign in His kingdom. Jesus, Himself, had made similar predictions. Among the more notable of these predictions is the one we can read today in Mark 9:1, wherein He predicted that "there be some of them that stand here which shall not taste of death till they have seen the kingdom of God come with power."

It is not difficult to understand why even some of Jesus' followers would be expecting the kingdom to come into existence at any time. It was at this time, and with this in mind, that, according to Matthew's account, a mother approaches Jesus with a request. According to Mark's account, her sons were the ones with the request.

There is no contradiction here. As is the case in a lot of families, when a parent knows that something is important to his or her children, it also becomes important to the parent(s). This was no doubt at least part of the reason that James and John and their mother asked Jesus about places of prominence in the kingdom. Specifically, the request was for one of the brothers to sit on the right hand of Jesus when He came into His kingdom (cf. Matt. 20:21, Mark 10:37).

The events that followed this question are interesting on some levels. As has already been mentioned briefly, there was a misunderstanding about the nature of the kingdom. While His followers then (and some professed followers now) were looking for a physical kingdom, Jesus would make it clear that "My kingdom is not of this world" (John 18:36).

It will be left to others to discuss all of the theological and doctrinal implications of the events and conversation we are considering. But there seems to be some material of a very practical nature.

THE DANGER OF JEALOUSY & ENVY

In the text we are considering, we get a glimpse of how easy it is for jealousy to rear its head, even among followers of Christ. As we continue reading the text, we find these words in Matthew 20:24, "And when the ten heard it [the conversation about the kingdom and places of prominence therein], they were greatly displeased with the two brothers." It appears to this observer that there must have been at least some degree of jealousy that caused this type of reaction among the other apostles. Otherwise, why would they have cared whether or not James and John received a positive answer to their request?

Jealousy and envy do not get much "good press" in God's Word. One interesting account is found in Genesis 30:1 where we read, "Now when Rachel saw that she bore Jacob no children, Rachael envied her sister, and said to Jacob, 'Give me children, or else I die.'" Interestingly enough, her request was, in some ways, similar to a part of the conversation that Jesus had with James and John. Subsequent events in Genesis demonstrate that Rachael died in childbirth. It could easily be argued that she got much more than she asked for and that what she got was not exactly what she had in mind.

Similarly, in the conversation with Jesus, James and John confidently affirmed that they were able to "drink the cup that [Jesus was] about to drink, and be baptized with the baptism that [Jesus was to be] baptized with" (Matt. 20:22). They, like Rachael, really did not understand all of the implications of what they were saying. The adage that suggests to us that we need to be careful what we ask for might well find some justification in these two passages.

In Genesis 37, we read about the envy of Joseph's brothers and how that envy led to them selling their own brother and allowing their father think that he was dead. Again, the negative effects of envy are on display.

This terrible emotion or attitude even played a major role in our Lord's crucifixion. Even Pilate could figure out why the Jews had brought Jesus to him. Matthew records that "he knew ... that they had handed Him over because of envy" (27:18).

If we believe that becoming a follower of Jesus automatically eliminates envy or jealousy, we might want to reconsider that in light of such passages as 1 Corinthians 3:1-3. The "babes in Christ" were being rebuked for remaining "carnal." One piece of evidence of this was envy.

The seriousness of this can be seen in the list of the "works of the flesh" in Galatians 5:19-21. Envy is listed right along with such things as murder, drunkenness, and adultery. Along with that, we are warned that "those who practice such things will not inherit the kingdom of God."

THE IMPORTANCE OF A PROPER EXAMPLE

I find it very interesting that Matthew 20:28 begins with the words "just as." Jesus was not asking his followers to do something He, Himself, was not willing to do. Rather, He was leading by example! This may be the best leadership "technique" there is.

I am convinced that a part of the reason why our society is struggling with some of the problems with which we are struggling is that some of our '"leaders" have led us in the wrong direction by their example. When politicians and pundits give lip service to such things as "family values" and the "Judeo-Christian ethic" while they live lives that are morally bankrupt and are never seen darkening the door of any kind of synagogue or church building, one has to wonder where their "values" and "loyalties" really are.

Elders in the Lord's church are charged with "being examples to the flock" (1 Pet. 5:3). What a harmonious and pleasant experience it is when a congregation of God's people knows they are being led and not pushed!

The importance and value of example can be seen at the family level as well. Repeatedly, the Bible teaches parents that their most important function lies in the area of the spiritual development of the children. Specifically, the husband, who is given the role as the head of the household, should be the spiritual leader of the family and should fulfill that role by setting the proper example. How many fathers have realized after it was far too late that they should have taken this responsibility more seriously instead of pursuing their careers, hobbies, etc.?

THE LORD DOES NOT VIEW THINGS LIKE WE DO

The words found in Isaiah 55:8-9 are probably familiar to most students of the Bible. The words recorded there are a clear statement that the way of the world is not God's way at all. "'For My thoughts are not your thoughts, Nor are My ways your ways,' says the Lord. 'For as the heavens are higher than the earth, So are My ways higher than your ways, And My thoughts than your thoughts.'"

The passage we are considering is another crystal clear example of this great truth. The world's view of greatness and our Lord's view of greatness could hardly be any more different. To those who think like the world, "greatness" is to be found in such things as money, power, prestige, titles, awards, etc. Many wait almost breathlessly for news about the next Oscar, Emmy, or Grammy winner. It is interesting that only a relatively short time after these (and other) awards are handed out, many of those same people have already forgotten who the winners were and are looking for "the next big thing."

Give yourself a little test. See how many people and/or productions you can name which have received some of the awards mentioned above. See if you can name the winners of such events as the Super Bowl, the World Series, and the NBA title for the past decade. How about the NCAA teams that finished in first place in football and basketball during the same period? Can you begin ten years ago and even name the presidents of our nation in order?

Jesus brushed aside all that the world considers great with these words: "You know that the rulers of the Gentiles lord it over them, and those who are great exercise authority over them. Yet it shall not be so among you, but whoever desires to become great among you, let him be your servant. And whoever desires to be first among you, let him be your slave—just as the Son of Man did not come to be served, but to serve and to give His life a ransom for many" (Matt. 20:25-28).

What is so "great" about service? Other than having a desire to fulfill a commitment to the Lord, why would anybody turn his or her back on fame, fortune, wealth, and power just to be a servant? I read the following surprising "headline" online by *Time* on August 23, 2013—

Helping Others Helps You to Live Longer

Consider this paragraph: "A new review of the health effects of volunteering found that helping others on a regular basis — like serving food in a soup kitchen or reading to the blind— can reduce early mortality rates by 22%, compared to those in people who don't participate in such activities." The author, Maia Szalavitz mentions the following as possible benefits of helping others (serving):

- Decreased rates of depression
- Increased sense of life satisfaction and well-being
- Increasing social contact and reducing loneliness; which in turn can help decrease the risk of:
    - High blood pressure
    - Heart attacks
    - Strokes
    - Dementia

Before leaving this section, please consider one more thought from Ms. Szalavitz: "But don't expect to reap the benefits of longevity after tossing a few coins in the next charity collection you encounter. It takes regular sacrifice of time and effort to engage the sense of reward that comes from volunteering..."[1]

1. The material quoted and alluded to above may be found at http://healthland.time.com/2013/08/23/helping-others-helps-you-to-live-longer/

SERVICE IS CHRIST-LIKE

Now that we have taken a brief look at why people in general might want to consider a life devoted to service, we need to think about why a Christian would want to do so. Are not Christians called to higher and nobler reasons for our actions than those who are not followers of Christ?

Being a servant may be the most Christ-like thing we ever do. We recognize the truth that Jesus "made Himself of no reputation, taking the form of a bondservant" when He voluntarily left heaven and came to earth. (cf. Phil. 2:7). He did not come as many of His day thought He should have come and as many of our day might believe would have been more effective. He did not come with pomp and ceremony and other trappings of worldly power and greatness. Instead, He came as a servant.

We might overlook the fact that, in a sense, Jesus still serves. As He presently sits at the Father's right hand, He is serving as the "one mediator between God and men, the Man Christ Jesus" (1 Tim. 2:5). Jesus is also described in this manner after His ascension to heaven: "we have an advocate with the Father, Jesus Christ the righteous" (1 John 2:1).

The writer of Hebrews speaks of His present service in this manner: "Therefore He is also able to save to the uttermost those who come to God through Him, since He always lives to make intercession for them" (Heb. 7:25). If it is obvious that our Lord's role while on earth involved service and that He is presently serving, shouldn't something be true about those who wear His name? Should it not be the case that they (we) also are servants?

We find evidence that this was, indeed, the case in the first century. Four writers of the New Testament introduced epistles they wrote as "bondservants." Paul did this twice (cf. Rom. 1:1; Tit. 1:1). James, Peter, and Jude all did this one time each (cf. Jas. 1:1; 2 Pet. 1:1; Jude 1).

The Holy Spirit could have inspired each of these writers to introduce themselves in much more flattering and impressive ways. Attention could have been called to a close relationship with the Lord. Maybe some mention could have been made of great strides in advancing the kingdom due to the efforts by one or more of these writers.

However, the focus of these introductions is on the lowliness of service. Can we not try to emulate these writers and our Lord in this?

While I can try to emulate Jesus by being a servant, the texts under consideration mention something that only He could do. We should be eternally grateful that He was willing to "give His life a ransom for many" (Matt. 20:28; Mark 10:48).

In keeping with the tone of this book, we will not get into a deep discussion of all of the implications of the word "ransom." Basically, the idea has to do with the act of paying some price and/or doing something in order to free a captive.

Most who read these words will readily recognize the fact that those who are outside of Christ are pictured as being captives of sin and/or the devil. Words like "servant," "slaves," etc. may be used, but the message is always the same. Although people living in sin and disobedience to God may believe themselves to be free, they are actually enslaved in the worst possible way.

There would not be too many today (at least those who are reading this) who would argue that they can find salvation by keeping the Old Testament Law. Most would understand that it is no longer in effect.

However, we might want to briefly consider another possibility. It might be tempting to fall into the trap of thinking that we can "be good enough" or, in some way, "earn" our salvation.

Before we fall into that trap, each of us needs to consider the following (as well as many other New Testament passages): "For we ourselves were also once foolish, disobedient, deceived, serving various lusts and pleasures, living in malice and envy, hateful and hating one another. But when the kindness and the love of God our Savior toward man appeared, not by works of righteousness which we have done, but according to His mercy He saved us, through the washing of regeneration and renewing of the Holy Spirit, whom He poured out on us abundantly through Jesus

Christ our Savior, that having been justified by His grace we should become heirs according to the hope of eternal life" (Tit. 3:3-7).

It is not about our goodness. It is about God's goodness and our response to Him!

At least one more factor needs to be considered here. The motivation behind any service or giving is a very important component of this discussion. If I am serving only because of a sense of duty, something may be missing in my understanding of the New Testament and my relationship with the Lord. If my service is motivated only by the hope of a future reward, there is still something lacking in my understanding.

The following words penned by Paul should cause us to look much higher than only a sense of duty and/or hope of a future reward: "And though I bestow all my goods to feed the poor, and though I give my body to be burned, but have not love, it profits me nothing" (1 Cor. 13:3).

I have not given all of my worldly goods away to feed the poor. I have not had to sacrifice my life because of my commitment to Jesus. I have, however, been called to a life of service motivated by love. The members of the Lord's church at Thessalonica were commended for their "work of faith, labor of love, and patience of hope in our Lord Jesus in the sight of God and Father" (1 Thess. 1:3).

Wouldn't it be wonderful if that could be said about every congregation today? Wouldn't it be wonderful if it could be said about every member of every congregation? Wouldn't it be wonderful if it could be said about that member I see when I look into a mirror? Am I able to truthfully say the following words from the pen of the apostle Paul? Am I ready to accept the challenge to serve and to give? "For the love of Christ compels ["controls," ESV] us, because we judge thus: that if One died for all, then all died; and He died for all, that those who live should live no longer for themselves, but for Him who died for them and rose again" (2 Cor. 5:14-15).

11

"I HAVE COME AS A LIGHT INTO THE WORLD, THAT WHOEVER BELIEVES IN ME SHOULD NOT ABIDE IN DARKNESS"

JOHN 12:46

As we come to read the events recorded in the twelfth chapter of John, we are reading events that happen very shortly before the crucifixion of our Lord. In fact, just a few verses prior to the ones reproduced above, He has once again predicted His death (cf. John 12:27-36).

Sadly, we also find these words in verse 37: "But although He had done so many signs before them, they did not believe in Him." The confrontations with some of the Jewish leaders would continue right up to (and even after) the events of that fateful day when He was "lifted up" (v. 32). Even at this late date, the prophecy of Isaiah was recalled that predicted a hardening of the hearts and blindness in the understanding of those who should have accepted the Messiah (cf. John 12:39-41, Matt. 13:14-15, Isa. 6:9-10).

What may be even more disappointing and tragic are the words we read that inform us that there were those who did believe, but whose belief stopped at that point. John's record states this in John 12:42-43: "Nevertheless even among the rulers many believed in Him, but because of the Pharisees they did not confess Him, lest they should be put out of the synagogue; for they loved the praise of men more than the praise of God." It is of more than passing interest to consider, at least briefly, what some proponents of the concept of "faith only" salvation have to say about this passage of scripture. Brother James Burton Coffman, in his *Commentary on the Gospel of John* (p. 305), has the following quotations from some of these men. Among those quotations, we find the following:

- "A rational conviction ... but not a saving trust."
- "But they had no true faith in God."
- "It does not appear that they had a living, active faith, but that they were convinced in their understanding that he was the Messiah."
- "These rulers, not believing with the heart, did not make an open confession."

This author grew up in a religious denomination that taught (and still teaches) that salvation comes by faith alone. Baptism was a requirement for membership into that particular organization and they did insist on immersion as the "mode" of baptism, but one's baptism had nothing to do with his or her salvation. It was made very clear to me from the time I was old enough to understand anything that I was being taught that my personal belief in Jesus was the one and only real requirement. Further, I was taught that there is a world of difference between believing on Jesus and believing in Jesus.

Although I do not remember a specific sermon or Bible class that taught this, I'm sure that the text we are considering was used to support that idea. The only translation of the Bible I can remember anybody using when I was a child was the King James Version. Its rendering of John 12:42 says that "among the chief rulers also many believed on him."

There were those being taught in that religious group then (as I'm sure they are being taught now) that there is a vast difference in what is said about these Jewish rulers and what is said in John 3:16. Again, from the King James translation, we find these words in this popular verse: "For God so loved the world, that he gave his only begotten Son, that whosoever believeth in him should not perish, but have everlasting life."

The phrase, "believeth in him" in John 3:16, is translated from the following: *pisteúoon eis autón*. It is my understanding that the phrase, "believed on him" in John 12:42 is translated from *epísteusan eis autón*. Other than the tense of the verb "believe," there is no difference.

It would appear, then, that belief (at least as understood by many) is not sufficient to please the Lord. The following words of our Lord seem to be pretty clear about the role of confessing Him before others: "Therefore whoever confesses Me before men, him will I also confess before My Father who is in heaven. But whoever denies Me before men, him will I also deny before My Father who is in heaven" (Matt. 10:32-33).

With that being the case, it would be difficult to successfully argue that the religious leaders mentioned in John 12:42-43 could be considered in any sense in a covenant relationship with Jesus. Sadly, that same thing may be true of many in our day and time.

Since we have already discussed, at least briefly, some material having to do with both judging and salvation as these subjects relate to our Lord's purpose for coming to the earth, we will not deal with them here. We will deal with something that may be somewhat overlooked in this narrative. It may also be overlooked in some religious circles today, but it should not be.

The material in John 12:42-43 gives us a glimpse into the problem of religious intimidation. This is not the first time the gospel of John provides us with information about those who either were intimidated or were the targets of such actions.

For example, we read in John 7 about the officers who had been sent out by the Jews to arrest Jesus. When they came back "empty-handed," they were, indeed, the targets of this type of tactic by the Jewish leaders. In John 9, the parents of the blind man who had been healed by Jesus and the man himself were the subjects of intimidation. Interestingly, it appears that the parents succumbed to this tactic for the same reason that some of the people written about in John 12 succumbed to it; they were afraid of being put out of the synagogue.

What was the goal of the "truth squads" sent out by the Jews as the early Christians spread the gospel? When we read about the efforts of these people, we are reading once again about a form of religious intimidation.

Sadly, this is still happening today. Our society in many subtle (and some not so subtle) ways tries to get those who have any sort of belief in Jesus to feel as though they are backward, uneducated, out of touch, etc. People lose promotions in business and industry daily because of their religious convictions. Far too many feel as though they have to make a choice between making a real contribution to society and being a Christian.

Our schools today are hotbeds of religious intimidation. Our young people are bombarded with lifestyles and philosophies that are completely antithetical to living a Christian life and following the teaching of our Master. They are given the very clear impression that only the "losers" and the "ignorant" would accept the Bible and its instruction about anything.

Religious intimidation also exists in the religious world. When did the word "fundamentalist" become such a disparaging term? When did it become unusual to call oneself a Christian and, at the same time, stand for such things as the inerrancy of God's Word, accepting the Bible as one's only standard of authority, the Deity of Jesus, the absolute necessity to worship God in the manner He chooses (not us), the need to be members of the church Jesus promised to build and over which He is the head, etc.?

Before we start pointing fingers at others, we would do well to consider that many forms of religious intimidation still exist among those who worship with a group of people who identify themselves collectively as a church of Christ. How often among those congregations has something been done just because it had the support of some "influential brethren;" or the elders approved it; or somebody was "shouted down" in a meeting; or because of a fear of losing a certain group (the young people, the "good givers," etc.); or for a number of other reasons that really all boil down to the idea that somebody "loved the praise of men more than the praise of God"?

Am I the only person who has heard somebody complain about having a "Diotrephes" in a local congregation? Before I get myself in too much trouble, I hasten to add that I am not writing about the congregation where I preach or any individual in that congregation. At the same time, I've been around long enough and have heard often enough that Diotrephes has some spiritual descendants. I recently heard a brother describe Diotrephes as one who accepted what God excluded and excluded those whom God accepted.

Does that not sound familiar? Are there not those who will use their position in a local congregation (elder, preacher, treasurer, etc.), the amount of their contribution, their family and/or brotherhood connections, or any host of other things to intimidate others into submission? It might be a good idea to spend some time with the second chapter of Galatians. Paul writes here of two occasions when he "stood up to" people. In both instances, he could have easily succumbed to religious intimidation.

First, Paul had to deal with "false brethren secretly brought in" (v. 4). Paul's reaction was dramatic and emphatic. He wrote that "we did not yield submission for an hour" (v. 5). It could be argued that Paul should not have had to worry about intimidation since he was an apostle and his antagonists are identified as false brethren. It could also be suggested that this could be seen as a confrontation between a relatively new Christian and those who at least purported to have been Christians for quite some time. One wonders how many "babes in Christ" have lost their enthusiasm and/or have gone into religious error or back into the world because some older and more experienced "brethren" have intimidated those precious souls.

While one may wonder about the validity of any religious intimidation in that scene, there is no doubt about the possibility of religious intimidation in the second incident to which Paul refers in Galatians 2. It will be remembered that this is the chapter wherein we read about his confrontation with Peter. Religious intimidation is at least suggested in various ways as these events unfold.

We remember that Paul identified himself as an apostle who was "born out of due time" and "the least of the apostles, who am not worthy to be called an apostle" (1 Cor. 15:8-9). Is it not possible that he could have felt intimidated by one of the original twelve apostles? Whether Peter was inclined to "throw his weight around" or not, it seems entirely possible that the mere presence of an original apostle who was part of the "inner circle" of apostles, and who was the chief spokesman could be intimidating.

None of that mattered to Paul. Rather than being intimidated by Peter, we read these words: "Now when Peter had come to Antioch, I withstood him to his face because he was to be blamed" (Gal. 2:11).

As we dig a little deeper into this account, we may gain even more insight into the problem of religious intimidation. What was Peter doing that was so wrong? Why was he doing that which was so wrong? The answer to the first question is fairly easy. He was conducting himself differently in different circumstances. This was especially true about those with whom he would associate.

As we read in verse 12, he was associating with Gentiles "before certain men came from James" When those Jews showed up, however, he "withdrew and separated himself" Was Peter intimidated by them? Was he concerned about what his Jewish brethren thought? Was he letting them control his actions in spite of what he preached in Acts 2 and practiced in Acts 10-11?

The answer to all of those questions could very well be an emphatic "Yes." That is spelled out for us in verse 12 as we learn that Peter acted the way he did because he was "fearing those who were of the circumcision."

If Peter could be intimidated in that way, I'm wondering how easy it is for me to be intimidated in similar circumstances. Do I let others dictate my actions; even when I know better?

Let's peel another layer off of this account in Galatians 2. Not only did Peter let the opinion of others dictate his actions, his actions influenced others to the extent that "the rest of the Jews also played the hypocrite with him" (v. 13). What would you do if you were in the presence of an apostle? Would you act as he acted?

Again, while I find no evidence that Peter demanded others to follow him in this practice, the fact remains that they did. The mere presence of a "church leader" may intimidate others.

It is of more than passing interest to notice that one of the people influenced by all of this was none other than "the son of encouragement." Sadly, even Barnabas went along with all of this.

Before we leave this discussion, we need return to what is intended to be the major thrust of this book. Somehow all of this discussion needs to "tie in" with a reason for our Lord's coming to live on the earth.

The "tie in" is in verses 5, 14. Others may be concerned about things that can (and do) intimidate. As stated in those two verses in Galatians 2, Paul's concern was for "the truth of the gospel." By definition, the gospel is the good news about Jesus. That was Paul's concern. That should be our concern as well. It is my prayer that we will let no circumstance and no person intimidate us into a failure to stand up for Him and proclaim His truth. It was our Lord who said, "And do not fear those who kill the body but cannot kill the soul. But rather fear Him who is able to destroy both soul and body in Hell" (Matt. 10:28).

12

"FOR THIS CAUSE I HAVE COME INTO THE WORLD, THAT I SHOULD BEAR WITNESS TO THE TRUTH"

JOHN 18:37

We have now come to the point in our Lord's earthly ministry when He was standing before Pilate. The Jewish leaders, of course, were the ones who made sure that He was tried by Pilate. They also took great measures to make sure that they kept (at least what in their own minds) was the "letter of the law." John 18:28 is, to me, a very interesting verse. It provides invaluable insight into the thinking of these leaders (and maybe the thinking of many people today). This verse informs us that, while they led him to the Praetorium, "they themselves did not go into the Praetorium, lest they should be defiled, but that they might eat the Passover."

Think of it! The very ones who would leave no stone unturned to put to death the Messiah wanted to make sure that they did not miss out on participating in an important religious observance. Did they really think that the Passover, as important as it was and as Divinely ordained as it was, would somehow shield them from the guilt of the greatest miscarriage of justice ever known? Were they so caught up in ceremony and observance that they thought that their "ticket was punched" no matter what else they did?

If those questions could be answered in the affirmative, there remains another question to consider. Could it possibly be that there are people like them living in our time?

Could I suggest that the following people might spend some "quality time" in a little self-examination?

- The brother or sister who involves himself/herself in character assassination all week long, but who is very careful to participate in the Lord's supper every Lord's day.
- The church member who makes sure that the amount of his or her financial support of the local church is a generous proportion of the amount of money he or she has made during the preceding week, but who has obtained that money in questionable, fraudulent, or immoral ways.
- The person who knows and uses every argument against the use of instrumental music in the worship of the Lord, but who uses his or her lips to sing "praises" to the Lord and to tell smutty stories and use foul language.
- The one who demands a "thus saith the Lord" for every activity, lesson, work, etc., but who cannot be trusted to keep his word.

The list could go on and on, but you get the idea. Religious ceremony did not then, nor does it now, by itself ensure that our relationship with the Lord is what it needs to be. We need to remember Jesus' denunciation of the scribes and Pharisees in Matthew 23:23-24: "Woe to you, scribes and Pharisees, hypocrites! For you pay tithe of mint and anise and cummin, and have neglected the weightier matters of the law: justice and mercy and faith. These you ought to have done, without leaving the others undone. Blind guides, who strain out a gnat and swallow a camel!"

The events recorded in John 18 also demonstrate a common "tactic" used by many when they do not really have an argument. When the Jewish leaders were asked what the charges against Jesus were, their response was, "If He were not an evildoer, we would not have delivered Him up to you" (v. 30).

Can you not hear the echoes of those today who, when questioned about some accusations they may have made, will respond, "Are you calling me a liar?" Apparently, they think that settles the issue. I don't know about you, but I'd much rather hear reason than bluster!

Of course, we all know the adage that suggests, "Where there's smoke, there's fire." Often it is accepted as true. Even in our society, this adage will overrule our system of law that is supposed to allow a person to be thought of as innocent until he or she is proven guilty. Can we not see this type of thinking in John 18:35? Although the Jews had not provided Pilate with any real evidence that proved that Jesus deserved to die, he seemed to think there was some sort of "fire" that cause the "smoke" of their charges when he said to Jesus, "Your own nation and the chief priests have delivered You to me. What have you done?"

Again, there are echoes of that type of thinking in the minds of many people today. Sadly, this is sometimes true even in the church. In spite of the fact that love "believes all things" (1 Cor. 13:7), some get their exercise by jumping to conclusions. I am personally aware of some good brothers and sisters who are serving the Lord in a variety of ways, but who have clouds of suspicion over their heads. People who do not know all the facts about certain matters nevertheless believe that they do and quietly spread what they mistakenly believe is the truth in order to "keep the church pure." They might be more than a little surprised about the context of Paul's admonition to the effect that "if anyone does not obey our word in this epistle, note that person and do not keep company with him, that he may be ashamed." (2 Thess. 3:14). In the immediate context, Paul is writing about "busybodies" (v. 11).

The material in John 18-19, of course, is one of those places where we learn about somebody who failed to live up to what he knew to be true. Twice Pilate announced that he could find no fault in our Lord (cf. John 18:38; 19:4).

However, because of "political pressure," popular opinion, and some other factors, Pilate did not act on his convictions. If, in fact, he had the power to crucify Jesus and the power to release Him (cf. John 19:10), why did he not release Him?

The answer to that question becomes painfully obvious when we consider people today who fail to act on their professed belief that Jesus is, indeed, the Son of God and/or that the doctrinal stance of the church of Christ in the twenty-first century is the same as the doctrinal stance of the church of Christ in the first century. Family pressures, political or social concerns, and many other factors still keep far too many people from acting on what they know to be right.

It is interesting that an important part of the discussion between Jesus and Pilate had to do with the nature of the kingdom of Christ and whether or not He claimed to be a king. It almost looks as though our Lord changed the subject or had ignored altogether what Pilate had asked Him about what He had done when He made the following statement: "My kingdom is not of this world. If my kingdom were of this world, My servants would fight, so that I should not be delivered to the Jews; but now my kingdom is not from here" (John 18:36).

It is always a valuable study to consider some of the prophecies made in both the Old and New Testaments concerning the kingdom over which the Messiah would reign. Volumes have been written about those prophecies and their fulfillment in the person of Jesus and His ownership and control of His church.

It will not be our purpose here to look in detail at all of those prophecies and whether or not they have been fulfilled. Our discussion of this point will be fairly brief.

Surely, a student of the gospels has noticed that both John the Baptist and our Lord challenged their listeners to "Repent, for the kingdom of heaven is at hand" (Matt. 3:2; 4:17). If something is "at hand," one would expect it to happen very soon, not thousands of years later.

In addition to that, Mark 9:1 records Jesus saying, "there are some standing here who will not taste death till they have seen the kingdom of God present (having come, margin) with power." Either the kingdom came into existence a long time ago, or there are some people alive today who would make Methuselah look like a tyke.

Without entering into a more detailed study of this point, suffice it to say that it is my firm conviction that the prophecies concerning the kingdom's beginning were fulfilled by the unusual events which occurred on the day of Pentecost as recorded in Acts 2. After that important day, the kingdom is spoken of as already being in existence, not as something to be anticipated as future events unfolded.

For example, Colossians 1:13-14 informs the reader that "He [God] has delivered us from the power of darkness and conveyed us into the kingdom of the Son of His love, in whom we have redemption through His blood, the forgiveness of sins." This same truth can be seen in such passages as 1 Thessalonians 2:12 and Hebrews 12:22-24, 28. In addition to these (and other) passages, the fact that John was in the kingdom when he wrote the book of Revelation should not be overlooked (cf. Rev. 1:9).

The statement made by our Lord in John 18:36 also suggests something about the nature of the kingdom. Jesus very clearly states that His kingdom is not like most concepts one would think of when the subject of a kingdom comes to mind.

While there may be many differences among the kingdoms of the world concerning economic policy, social issues, etc., there is usually one point of similarity among all (or at least most) of them. Most kingdoms have some sort of military and/or police component in place. While only a few kingdoms, thankfully, have demonstrated a desire to attack and control other nations and people, most kingdoms at least make sure that they have the ability to defend themselves, their territory, and/or their leader(s).

Jesus indicated that this was not at all the case with His kingdom or His followers. His statement, "if My kingdom were of this world, My servants would fight, so that I should not be delivered to the Jews" (John

18:36), is a clear indication that His kingdom was, indeed, different; at least in this respect.

The people who had heard Jesus teach during His ministry should have already known that His (and His Father's) plans for His kingdom were different from any other kingdom ever known. All one has to do today is to read the material found in Matthew 13 to get this idea.

In Matthew 13, Jesus made repeated comparisons concerning His kingdom. First, He compares the kingdom to a man who sows seed on various types of soil. Following that comparison and His explanation of it, He said six times that "the kingdom of heaven is like" something:

- The kingdom of heaven is like a man who sowed good seed in his field (v. 24)
- The kingdom of heaven is like a mustard seed (v. 31)
- The kingdom of heaven is like leaven (v. 33)
- Again, the kingdom of heaven is like treasure hid in a field (v. 44)
- Again, the kingdom of heaven is like a merchant man seeking beautiful pearls" (v. 45)
- Again, the kingdom of heaven is like a dragnet that was cast into the sea (v. 47)

One very apparent common element in all of these comparisons is the absolute lack of any imagery of a military or political nature. Nothing in these parables suggests the type of kingdom that most people would have had in mind.

Of course, another clue to the unusual nature of His kingdom is to be found in conversation He had with the Pharisees as recorded in Luke 17:20-21: "Now when He was asked by the Pharisees when the kingdom of God would come, He answered them and said, 'The kingdom of God does not come with observation; nor will they say, 'See here!' or 'See there!' For indeed, the kingdom of God is within you.'"

The marginal reading of the KJV and the NKJV, as well as other translations, may help us to better understand the phrase, "within you." In these places, the rendering is "within your midst" or "in the midst of you." These Pharisees, who were looking for an earthly kingdom which they thought was to come in the future, were talking at that time to the king.

It is not the design of this chapter or of this book to involve ourselves in a thorough study of the doctrine of premillennialism. Others have done this and have shown some of the fallacies of that theory. However, it might be helpful to make one point before we leave this part of our discussion. We have already briefly demonstrated earlier in this chapter that the kingdom that both John the Baptist and Jesus said was "at hand" did, in fact, come into existence during the time in which the New Testament was being written.

An argument that may serve as a corollary to the suggestion that the kingdom is not now in existence is that Jesus did, indeed, intend to establish a kingdom when He came to the earth and that He did, in fact, say that it was at hand. According to this theory, He must have overestimated the willingness of the Jews to accept Him as a king. Since (according to the theory) He was rebuffed in His plans, He decided to have the church come into existence as a sort of temporary substitute until He can return the second time to establish that kingdom.

There are many flaws in that idea. One obvious flaw has to do with the validity and power of Jesus. How can we be sure that Jesus will succeed the second time if He failed the first time? Along with that, we wonder if He should be accepted as Lord in any sense if He failed so miserably at something this important.

In addition to that, it is not true that the Jews rejected the idea that He could be an earthly king. On the contrary, after miraculously feeding the 5,000 with five barley loaves and two fish, "Jesus perceived that they were about to come and take Him by force to make Him king, He departed again to the mountain by Himself alone" (John 6:15).

Jesus was very aware of the "timing" in God's plan concerning the kingdom. Statements like "My time has not yet come" and "My time has not yet fully come" (John 7:6, 8) show this to be true.

Even after His resurrection and very close to the events recorded in Acts 2 (when the timing was right), Jesus refused to answer a question about the Divine timetable for the kingdom. At the same time, He indicated that there was, indeed, such a timetable, and He did give His apostles some clues to look for. All of this can be found in Acts 1:6-8: "Therefore, when they had come together, they asked Him, saying, 'Lord, will You at this time restore the kingdom to Israel?' And He said to them, 'It is not for you to know times or seasons which the Father has put in His own authority. But you shall receive power when the Holy Spirit has come upon you; and you shall be witnesses to Me in Jerusalem, and in all Judea and Samaria, and to the end of the earth.'"

Not only was the timing wrong in John 6, the source of authority was also wrong. Sometimes, even today, we hear of individuals and/or groups of individuals referred to as "kingmakers." When "their man (or woman)" makes it to the desired position, there is always some question about where the real power lies. The person who has been put into an important position by others may be so beholden to them that, in reality, the "kingmakers" have the authority and power. Various political machines can serve as examples of this.

If Jesus had let the Jews force Him into being a king, He would, of necessity, have had to have been their kind of king. He would never have been able to make the claim the He had all authority or power (cf. Matt. 28:18). They, not the Lord, would have been "pulling the strings."

However, as one studies the New Testament, it becomes very apparent that Jesus was, in fact, in control of the entire situation. There is an important piece of information contained in John's record of the conversation between Pilate and the Jews in John 18:31-32: "Then Pilate said to them, 'You take Him and judge Him according to your law.' Therefore the Jews said to him, 'It is not lawful for us to put anyone to death,' that the saying of Jesus might be fulfilled which He spoke, signifying by what death He would die."

When this is considered along with other statements Jesus made, it is obvious that neither the Jews nor Pilate were in control. Our Lord was in complete control and, as He said, "I lay down my life that I may take it again. No one takes it from Me, but I lay it down of Myself. I have the power to lay it down, and I have the power to take it again" (John 10:17-18).

The fact that this was all part of God's plan for our redemption should not cause anybody to think that this eliminates any guilt on the part of those who were involved in sentencing Jesus to death and carrying out the execution. A part of the sermon we have recorded for us in Acts 2 should point this out to us.

In the same sentence, Peter declares that Jesus was "delivered by the determined purpose and foreknowledge of God" and that "you have taken [Him] by lawless hands, [and] have crucified, and put to death" (Acts 2:23). It was futile for Pilate or for any of the other people on that day to attempt to wash their hands and, thereby, seek to get rid of their guilt.

Not only did Jesus say that He came to be a king, but He also declared that He came to "bear witness to the truth" (John 18:37). Does that mean that Jesus, Himself, is not the truth, but that He could add credence to the truth?

If that is the case, what did He mean in John 14:6, wherein He declares Himself to be "the way, the truth, and the life"? There is an interesting answer to this tucked away neatly in John 5. In verse 31 of that chapter, Jesus is quoted as saying that John the Baptist had "borne witness to the truth."

As we compare that statement with John 1:15, it should be evident that John bore witness to a person, not a concept. Thus, our Lord is the embodiment of truth.

In passing, it is important to notice two other facts. First, the phrase "bear witness" is from the same Greek word as is the English word, "testify." Secondly, in the context of John 5, where it is said that John the Baptist had borne witness to the truth (Jesus), others are called upon who are said to "bear witness" or "testify" that Jesus' claims are true. First, Jesus indicates that He could testify for Himself, but acknowledges that this type of testimony might be rejected. Jesus declares that all of the following would support Him in His claims:

- John (v. 33)
- His works (v. 36)
- His Father (v. 37)
- the Scriptures (v. 39)

Jesus had already pointed out, in His teaching in John 10 about His relationship with His sheep, how His sheep hear His voice. In John 18, He says much the same thing in a slightly different way. In verse 37, He is quoted as saying, "Everyone who is of the truth hears my voice."

The fact that the same message about Jesus can have opposite effects on people is seen vividly in the events recorded in Acts 2 and Acts 7. In Acts 2, the message resulted in the conversion of thousands of people. In Acts 7, the same basic message resulted in the murder of the messenger. As Paul would later write: "For we are to God the fragrance of Christ among those who are being saved and among those who are perishing. To the one we are the aroma of death leading to death, and to the other the aroma of life leading to life. And who is sufficient for these things" (2 Cor. 2:15-16).

It is still true today that the message of the gospel has different effects on people. It is also still true today that a question raised in John 18 is still relevant.

In fact, there are two questions that are raised which are relevant. One is Pilate's question, "What is truth?" (John 18:38). Our postmodern world would do well to deal with that question.

We are being told today that there is no such thing as absolute truth. It would be profitable for those who propose this type of thinking and for those who have "bought into it" to be confronted with the absolute truth that there is, indeed, absolute truth!

However, for the purpose of this study, it might be just as helpful and maybe more thought-provoking to consider a question asked by Jesus. When Pilate asked Him if He was the King of the Jews (v. 33), our Lord's response was, "Are you speaking for yourself about this, or did others tell you this concerning Me?"

That's a question that still "hangs in the air" for me and for all of us. Each one of us needs to consider whether our faith and commitment to the Lord is personal. When I (we) make statements concerning the authority of Christ, are those statements merely academic or theological statements? Am I just parroting what I've heard others say or what I know I'm supposed to say?

Pilate tried to shift the blame to others; he literally washed his hands; he tried other measures to attempt to absolve himself of any responsibility for the Lord's crucifixion. All such efforts were in vain.

All such efforts are still in vain. The truth remains that "we must all appear before the judgment seat of Christ, that each one may receive the things done in the body, according to what he has done, whether good or bad" (2 Cor. 5:10).

13

"NOW I AM COME TO YOU ... THAT THEY MAY HAVE MY JOY FULFILLED IN THEMSELVES"

JOHN 17:13

For the first time in this volume, we are intentionally moving backward in time. The statement from the lips of our Lord reproduced above is not the last statement He made about His mission. In fact, unlike the other statements we have considered, it is not, in itself, a statement as to why He came to earth. It is, rather, a statement made to His Father about His return to the glory He had with the Father before He left heaven to come to earth (cf. John 17:5).

Many will recognize this text as a portion of what truly should be considered as a part of the "Lord's Prayer." Unlike the "Model Prayer" found in Matthew 6:9-13 and Luke 11:2-4, the words found in John 17 clearly and forcefully express our Lord's innermost feelings as He approaches His sacrificial death on the cruel cross.

Without going into a detailed study of the prayer, itself, we can notice that it is divided into three main sections. In verses 1-5, Jesus is found to be praying about His mission. In verses 6-19, the focus is on His apostles. It is humbling and challenging to read verses 20-26 because Christians of every age are included in this portion of the prayer. When we read the words in verse 20 about "those who will believe in Me through their word," does not that include even those living today?

As we study this prayer, we can catch a glimpse of the eternal nature of Deity. Specifically, we are reminded that God is not limited by the confines of time, either in His actions or His thinking, unless He chooses to put Himself on a "timetable" in order for mankind to see that God's will was being carried out exactly as He planned.

It was for man's benefit, not God's, that we read statements such as, "But when the fullness of the time had come, God sent forth His Son, born of a woman, born under the law, to redeem those who were under the law, that we might receive the adoption of sons" (Gal. 4:4). The entire scheme of redemption, including the establishment of the church, was "according to the eternal purpose which He accomplished in Christ Jesus our Lord" (Eph. 3:11).

In a manner of speaking, when we are talking about any of the members of the Godhead, tense makes no sense. This can be seen in some of the statements made by Jesus in the prayer recorded in John 17.

Notice, for example, verse 4, where Jesus said to His Father, "I have glorified You on the earth. I have finished the work which you have given me to do." Remember, this was before the cross and before He would say, "It is finished" (John 19:30). From our vantage point, His work was not quite yet completed, but His expression made it sound as though it was already accomplished.

Another striking example of this is in John 17:11. In this verse, He is quoted as saying, "I am no longer in the world." How could that be? This cannot even be explained away by the fact that there might be some difference between how He appeared before the cross and after His resurrection. Again, this was said before His crucifixion.

Some have suggested that when God told Moses to tell the children of Israel that "I AM has sent me to you" (Exod. 3:14), he was using the "eternal present tense." It is of much more than mere casual interest that Jesus told some Jews in John 8:58, "(B)efore Abraham was, I AM." He thus identified Himself with the Father and gave them (and us) some insight into His eternal nature.

One verse in the book of Romans also gives us invaluable insight into God's eternal nature and the fact that He is not bound by the constraints of time. In the midst of a discussion about God's promise to Abraham and how that relates to our relationship with God, Paul is inspired to write the following: "(as it is written, 'I have made you a father of many nations') in the presence of Him whom he believed—God, who gives life to the dead and calls those things which do not exist as though they did" (Rom. 4:17).

Notice that both an example and explanation are given. The example is that before Abraham ever had any children, God used the past tense in saying, "I have made you a father of many nations." The explanation is that God "calls those things which do not exist as though they did." In short, our God is not bound by time (or space for that matter).

The remainder of this chapter will focus on what I believe to be some important components of this prayer. We hope, in the next few pages, to get a glimpse of the mind of Christ, the message of Christ, and the mission of Christ.

THE MIND OF CHRIST

The mind of Christ is what Paul instructs Christians to imitate in Philippians 2:5-8: "Let this mind be in you which was also in Christ Jesus, who, being in the form of God, did not consider it robbery to be equal with God, but made Himself of no reputation, taking the form of a bondservant, and coming in the likeness of men. And being found in appearance as a man, He humbled Himself and became obedient to the point of death, even the death of the cross." From this reading, and from other readings, we get the very clear picture that the mind of Christ was characterized by at least three attributes which are foreign to the thinking and practice of many of our day.

First, our Lord set the example of—and placed a great deal of emphasis on—humility. The One who "humbled Himself" expects His followers to do no less. Matthew quotes Jesus as saying on one occasion, "And whoever exalts himself will be humbled, and he who humbled himself will be exalted" (Matt. 23:12). Luke quotes Jesus as saying those same words in two places (cf. Luke 14:11; 18:14).

Matthew recorded one other incident when Jesus spoke about humility. The setting for this is interesting and instructive. The Lord's disciples were concerned about His concept of greatness. Specifically, they asked, "Who is greatest in the kingdom of heaven?" (Matt. 18:1).

It was at this point that Jesus used a child as an "object lesson." After calling the child to Him and "setting him in the midst of them" (Matt. 18:2), the Lord said: "Assuredly, I say to you, unless you are converted and become as little children, you will by no means enter the kingdom of heaven. Therefore whoever humbles himself as this little child is the greatest in the kingdom of heaven" (Matt. 18:3-4).

Jesus had little use for those of His day who "say and do not do" (Matt. 23:3). I suppose that a modern equivalent of that would be those about whom it may be accurately said that they "talk the talk, but do not walk the walk." Jesus did not preach what He did not practice. The passage quoted above links His humility with His obedient sacrifice on the cross, but that one reference encompasses an entire earthly existence characterized by humility.

In the sense of economic status, Jesus was born in humble circumstances to humble parents. He would also refer to His own "humility" in this sense by saying that He had "nowhere to lay His head" (Matt. 8:20; Luke 9:58). When the soldiers gambled for his clothing as He was being crucified, the inference is that they were gambling for the only earthly possession He had.

However, the type of humility being discussed here has much less to do with circumstances and much more to do with attitude and action. Have we not all been acquainted with people who are very poor by the standards of the world, but who, for some reason, exhibit an attitude of pride and arrogance? While that seems incongruous, it does happen from time to time.

At the same time, have we not also been acquainted with (or at least heard about) people of great material possession and/or social standing that are very humble and "down to earth" when one gets to know them? While it may be rare, those people do exist.

Maybe the following story will help to illustrate what I'm trying to "get at" here:

> In the United States, years ago, a party of soldiers was trying to pull out a wagon that was stuck in the mud. The Corporal in charge was urging them on. But the wagon was very heavy and the mud was very thick. A passer-by stopped to talk to the corporal. The corporal complained to him: "They give me six men only to do the work of ten," "Why don't you lend your men a hand yourself?" asked the stranger. The corporal looked shocked, "But, I'm the Corporal," he said. The stranger said no more; he took off his coat and set his shoulder to one of the wheels of the wagon. With this help, the soldiers managed to get the wagon out of the muck. As he put on his coat, the stranger turned to the corporal. "When you need help again, Corporal, call on the Commander-in-Chief," he said. He was none other than George Washington himself, the first President and Commander-in-Chief of the army of the United States of America.[1]

Our Lord was not humble merely because of His circumstances, nor did He merely talk about humility. One incident as recorded in one chapter in one of the Gospels should be enough to forcefully demonstrate this to be true. I encourage those who are reading these words to pause for a moment; pick up a Bible; and turn to the thirteenth chapter of John.

---

1. https://www.yumpu.com/en/document/view/18159108/but-im-the-corporal-the-story

Who is the One in John 13 exhibiting humility as He washes the dirty, smelly feet of mere men? Who is the One washing the feet of the one who will deny any knowledge of Him later? Who is the One washing the feet of the man who will sell Him for thirty pieces of silver? Who is the One treating all of these men alike? I suggest that the scene described in John 13 should serve as the example for those who would follow Him. In fact, that is not my suggestion. A reading of verses 12-17 of that same chapter will inform us that Jesus intends for His followers to follow his example and His teaching about humility.

A second characteristic of the mind of Christ that is mentioned in Philippians 2 is obedience. Consider carefully the message and importance of the following words: "though He was a Son, yet He learned obedience by the things which He suffered. And having been perfected, He became the author of eternal salvation to all who obey Him" (Heb. 5:8-10).

The message is clear, and the importance is obvious. For me to have the "mind of Christ," I must be obedient. In fact, in order to be with Him in heaven, I must be obedient.

The concept of obedience is foreign to many of our day. It does not matter whether we are talking about family relationships, societal and legal issues, or our relationship with God. The fact is that people minimize and/or deny that obedience is necessary in any way.

In religious circles, we sometimes hear the argument that a person cannot obey the gospel. The "reasoning" goes something like this. The word "gospel" means "good news." How, we are asked, can anybody obey good news? We might accept good news, appreciate it, and spread it, but it cannot be obeyed—or so the thinking goes. How do we answer that? Our answer is found in 2 Thessalonians 1:7-8. Please consider carefully these words: "And to give you who are troubled rest with us when the Lord Jesus is revealed from heaven with His mighty angels, in flaming fire taking vengeance on those who do not know God, and on those who do not obey the gospel of our Lord Jesus Christ."

There is a third concept found in Philippians 2 which is just as important as the other two in order for me to have the mind of Christ. That concept is just as unpopular and possibly just as rare as the other two. Although the word is not used, the concept of service permeates the passage. Since we have discussed this in an earlier chapter, we will not belabor the point here. Suffice it to say that, if I am to have the mind of Christ, I must be a humble and obedient servant.

THE MESSAGE OF CHRIST

As we return to the prayer in John 17, we find some interesting words that "hint at" the message of Christ. Speaking primarily of His apostles, He prays, "They are not of this world" (v. 16). As the prayer is expanded to include all people everywhere, the Lord prayed that "they [we] might be with Me where I am" (v. 16).Is there not a word for what we are considering here? Is not that word salvation?

It is again the case that we have discussed this earlier. For that reason, we do not intend to spend a great deal of time again on this important subject. However, it needs to be remembered that the message of our Lord was not merely about reformation. Likewise, His interest was not in making people more religious.

As Peter would say to Jesus, "You have the words of eternal life" (John 6:68). While those who would speak for Jesus today might speak words that would help in so many areas of life, we would be most negligent if we did not focus on the salvation of our own souls and the souls of those who hear us.

As Paul wrote to Timothy, we must "take heed to yourself and to the doctrine. Continue in them, for in doing this you will save both yourself and those who hear you" (1 Tim. 4:16).

One other concept needs to be mentioned here. Our Lord prayed about sanctification in John 17:17. As one studies the New Testament, it should become obvious that He did not have in mind some sort of "second work of grace" as is it is taught in some circles.

Simply put, the concept requires His followers to be different from the world. As He prayed on this occasion, people are sanctified by means of the word of God, which is the truth of God. That, in itself, would meet the requirement that God's people are different from anybody else in the world. We are to be "set apart" and that just happens to be the basic meaning of sanctification. As the Holy Spirit inspired Paul to write: "'Come out from among them And be separate,' says the Lord. 'Do not touch what is unclean, And I will receive you.' I will be a Father to you, And you shall be My sons and daughters, Says the Lord Almighty'" (2 Cor. 6:17-18).

THE MISSION OF CHRIST

How would one describe the overall earthly mission of our Lord? Thus far, we have discussed various facets of that mission, but what would be a good description of His overall mission?

It might be that the best place to go to do that would be to read a passage that gives us invaluable insight. It is as though we are allowed to eavesdrop on a conversation between the Father and the Son during which the Son says: "Sacrifice and offering You did not desire, But a body You have prepared for Me. In burnt offerings and sacrifices for sin You had no pleasure.' Then I said, 'Behold, I have come — In the volume of the book it is written of Me — To do Your will, O God'" (Heb. 10:5-7).

There it is! There is the best and most succinct description of the mission of Christ I know of anywhere. All that has been written up to this point and all that could be written would fit under the umbrella of our Lord's overarching mission. Please read it again: "I have come...to do Your will, O God."What higher calling could there be for us? What purpose in life could be nobler than that? What could give a greater sense of purpose?

"Wait," somebody might say, "The verse with which you began this chapter had to do with joy. What kind of joy is to be found in a life of obedience, service, humility, and some of the other things discussed here?

We will return to Hebrews for an answer to that: "Therefore we also, since we are surrounded by so great a cloud of witnesses, let us lay aside every weight, and the sin which so easily ensnares us, and let us run with endurance the race that is set before us, looking unto Jesus, the author and finisher of our faith, who for the joy that was set before Him endured the cross, despising the shame, and has sat down at the right hand of the throne of God" (Heb. 12:1-2).

I am informed that the word translated "joy" in that passage can have a couple of interesting meanings. The word can mean "calmly happy" or "calm delight."

Look around. Who are the people you know who seem to be calmly happy? In what type of person do you see calm delight? Are they the ones who have mistaken worldly happiness for biblical joy? Are they the ones who are chasing after every new experience (maybe even a religious one), possession, relationship, etc.?

Is it not the case that the people who can be described as truly joyful people are those who quietly and faithfully serve the Lord? They do not need all of the hoopla. They have all they want (and more) in a faithful relationship with the Lord and with His family.

One of the themes of that prayer in John 17 is unity. Specifically, Jesus wants all of his followers to be one (cf. vv. 20-21). It seems that, if I have the mind of Christ; live by the message of Christ; and do my part in fulfilling the mission of Christ, I will go a long way in answering that prayer in my life and in the lives of others. That, it seems, will make for unity.

EPILOGUE

I cannot close this volume without a reminder, both to those who read this book and myself, of these words: "I will come again" (John 14:3). It is, indeed, true that our Lord came the first time as our Savior. It is also true that His second appearance will be as our judge (cf. 2 Cor. 5:10). It is my prayer that there might be something in this book that will be helpful as we prepare for His return.

— Jim Faughn

Paducah, Kentucky

67089441R00077

Made in the USA
Lexington, KY
02 September 2017